How to
Beat Your
Competitors

THE SUNDAY TIMES

How to Beat Your Competitors

SECOND EDITION

John G Fisher

KOGAN PAGE | *CREATING SUCCESS*

For Carol, Jonathan, Camilla and Charis

First published in 1996 as *How to Improve Performance Through Bench-marking*
Second edition published in 2000

Kogan Page Limited
120 Pentonville Road
London N1 9JN

© John G Fisher 1996, 2000

British Library Cataloguing in Publication Data

A CIP record for this book is available from the British Library.

ISBN 0 7494 3431 7

Cover design by DW Design, London
Typeset by Jean Cussons Typesetting, Diss, Norfolk
Printed and bound in Great Britain by Clays Ltd, St Ives plc

contents

to the reader

As an enlightened manager, the easy part is understanding the theory of benchmarking. Putting what you have learnt to practical use is the difficult bit. Paradoxically, it is often harder to introduce such concepts as benchmarking into a small or medium-size company than a big corporation simply because resources tend to be more stretched in smaller organisations. No one has time to learn a new way of working – the company is too busy establishing itself or maintaining its position in a competitive marketplace. So, to make a step change, the corporate learning process needs an internal 'champion' if a new way of doing things is going to be adopted. You are that champion.

Once you have absorbed the main principles, you need to consider who, how and when. Clearly, you need top-level commitment as many of the changes you will introduce will require considerable internal adjustment and a diversion of precious human and financial resources. You will need to keep the process alive by initiating the formation of various working groups, the instigation of research projects and the establishment of reporting procedures. You will need to be sensitive to corporate inertia and be constantly enthusiastic whenever benchmarking is discussed. If not, the initiative may well die, along with the future prosperity of your organisation.

That is a heavy burden to carry. But you cannot become a champion without the necessary stamina to help you carry that burden. If you think you have got the stamina and the enthusiasm to beat the competition on a regular basis and make your organisation the Best In Class, read on.

introduction

beating the best through benchmarking

A business that stands still is a business that is going backwards. Continual improvements in communication, technology and marketing mean that simply in order to survive, every business has to improve itself; or otherwise it will cease to function.

In recent years there have been many attempts to encourage organisations to be self-critical. Deming, Crosby, Conway and Ishikawa were the pioneers of quality systems checks which together came to be known as TQM (total quality management). Rank Xerox is credited with being the first company to undertake, in the early 1980s, a complete review of its quality systems, which resulted in a new type of business management. It was based on process improvement and comparisons with other organisations to discover 'best practice'. David Kearns, the then chief executive officer (CEO) of Rank Xerox, commented, 'Competitive benchmarking tells us where we have to go'. But what exactly is benchmarking?

The word 'benchmarking' has had some confusing press. There seem to be several interpretations ranging from pernickety, scientific calibration to vague comparisons of corporate achievement. Those who are moved to produce a definition usually include a reference to a process or quality standard. But most people interpret benchmarking as a financial comparison of competitive business performance. Benchmarking is all of these things and none of them, when taken in isolation. In essence, benchmarking is examining the critical activities of your business and comparing your performance in those critical areas with the performance of other businesses or within your own business.

But the information is not collected for idle amusement. The purpose of benchmarking is to establish points of measurement from which you can improve your corporate performance by changing the way you do things. It could be argued that most if not all companies do this to a greater or lesser extent. It is true that there are few businesses that do not compare their ratios and financial historical figures with those of their direct competitors. But on closer examination, the comparisons are usually too broad: sales, profits, number of outlets, market share, for example. Even worse, the comparisons are not contemporaneous. The Annual Report of every business is always at least four months out of date. In addition, looking at figures over the 12 months of a financial year do not reveal much about how the business achieved what it did. We can only make educated guesses. At best we can only detect growth or decline. What you really need to have to improve the performance of your business is some knowledge of the key processes that makes one business so much better than its competitors.

One place to start could be your own organisation. There may be parts of your business that everyone admires because of their efficiency, the way they talk to internal customers or their general 'can-do' attitude. Benchmarking encourages organisations to borrow and adapt the best way of doing the same or similar tasks to everyone's satisfaction. But it does not only apply to huge corporations with dozens of subsidiaries. Even a small company can benefit. Does the way the marketing director communicates with the salesforce offer any ideas about how the production director should talk to his work teams? Could the warehouse team benefit from watching how the accounts department organises itself? Could the directors learn anything from the mailroom?

The next source is your competitors. What does the market leader do internally and externally that enables them to produce better quality at a lower price? Why do they always seem to be ahead of the game in new product development and marketing ideas? Why do they always seem to attract the best people? A few days analysing what makes them the best on the inside would do wonders for your own sales figures.

benchmarking: some definitions

Corporate life would be much more simple if each new business management concept came with a ready-made unequivocal definition. The truth is, however, that any concept worth having is multi-faceted. It needs to mean many things to different kinds of businesses if it is going to be taken seriously and last longer than a few months. The benchmarking concept is no exception. It can be the catalyst for extraordinary change, if its implications are fully understood.

In its sixth annual global study, published in July 2000, US consultancy Bain & Co ranked usage of management techniques to improve business performance across 475 large US and European companies. For Europe, benchmarking as a distinct technique was the *most used technique*, out of over 100 techniques mentioned by companies, for the last two years of the survey.

But what do people mean when they say they benchmark their performance? Rather than be dogmatic about defining what benchmarking is, it is worth considering several definitions or related techniques from a variety of sources, so that you can begin to understand the underlying elements of what could constitute sound benchmarking behaviour. No interpretation is any more valid than any other although each one reveals a little more about how the initial concept of comparison has been taken a stage further.

1. **Benchmarking, dictionary definition**
   A standard against which something can be measured. A survey mark of previously determined position used as a reference point.

2. **Benchmarking in the construction industry.**
   The ancient Egyptians were reputedly the first civilisation to use a rod of metal balanced in a wedge of stone block providing a 'level' from which others parts of the construction could be measured. The pyramids were constructed using benchmark readings.

3. **Shukko: Japanese concept of employee loan**
   In Japan certain employees are encouraged to study not only their own internal organisational processes but to learn from the internal processes of other companies, competitive or non-competitive, during special secondments. The benefits are the rapid transfer of best practice and technology (sometimes referred to as 'industrial tourism'). Benchmarking is based on studying and comparing work processes.

4. **Dr Mohamed Zairi, *Competitive Benchmarking*, 1988**
   'Anything taken or used as a point of reference or comparison. Something that serves as a standard by which others may be served; it is all to do with anything or something that is comparatively measurable.'

5. **Robert C Camp, Xerox Corporation, 1989**
   'Benchmarking is the search for and implementation of best practices ... The continuous process of measuring our products, services and practices against our toughest competitors or those companies known as leaders.'

6. *The Economist,* **reporting on a study of bench-marking by McKinsey, 1991**
   'The theory: by working closely with the best-performing firms, benchmarking teams can learn how to implement the processes and the skills needed to make their own company a world-beater.'

7. **Sylvia Codling, *Best Practice Benchmarking,* 1992**
   'Benchmarking is a rational, disciplined approach to continuous improvement which helps identify, compare with and emulate best practice wherever it occurs.'

8. **Royal Mail, UK, 1992**
   'A structural process for learning from the practice of others, internally or externally, who are leaders in a field or with whom legitimate comparisons can be made.'

9. **UK Department of Trade and Industry definition, 1995**
   'A systematic approach to business improvement where best practice is sought and implemented to improve a process beyond the benchmark performance.'

10. **Rob Reider, *Benchmarking Strategies,* 2000**
    'Benchmarking is concerned with continuously evaluating the company's best practices through internal and external comparisons.'

There are some common threads running through most of these definitions:

■ a point of reference for measurement;
■ a study of key internal processes;
■ comparison with other organisations;
■ continuous improvement;
■ to become the best.

Getting the benchmarking habit is about the careful analysis of how your internal organisation does what it does, how it adds value to raw materials or intellectual resources, how it matches market needs, and how it delivers the goods or service to the end customer.

four types of benchmarking

There are four generally accepted types of benchmarking that can be pursued, each with its own specific objectives.

1. internal benchmarking

Benchmarking the processes that your own organisation undertakes is usually where good benchmarking starts, because everyone can see it is in the organisation's best interests and, more critically, the information is to hand. The kind of questions the management should be asking are:

- What are our most admired procedures?
- What makes them efficient?
- What processes could be useful to other areas?
- What are we bad at?
- What makes such things inefficient?
- Why do we continue to do them?

Most new benchmarkers start this way and gain quick results, often wondering why they never did it before. But take care to tread carefully. Even in small companies, departmental sensitivities need to be respected. A consultative approach with adequate pre-visit explanations are essential to gain cooperation, not just for the first visit but for all the subsequent visits that would characterise a healthy benchmarking culture. The underlying measure for all your internal process changes should be whether a new way would deliver a better bottom line. This analysis is not always as simple as it looks, as many tasks that a company performs may not initially translate into tangible incremental profits. There may be disagreement about the value that such a change would add, both in absolute terms and in degree. The important point, though, is that the issue is being debated and things are changing.

Once the limited number of successful processes are copied within an organisation, what next? How do you improve if the processes being compared are now equally efficient? How do you overcome the strong urge to stop improving? And after a few months that 'we now do it this way' attitude is difficult to counteract, especially if the company is making good or adequate profits and no one internally can think of better ways to deliver customer satisfaction.

2. competitive benchmarking

One answer is to look beyond your own company. A direct competitor is usually the first place to look, particularly if that competitor seems to be doing better than you in the same marketplace. On the assumption that corporate ethics prevent industrial espionage, meaningful information about the internal processes of a competitor is not easy to acquire. In most cases it will be historic if published in trade or professional books and magazines. The chances are that the quoted process has been considerably improved by the time it reaches published status. The raw data and detailed analysis can only be acquired with a site visit and specific discussions with those operating the process. Such access is not likely to be granted by a direct competitor. Even if you were able to debrief new employees, hotfoot from their last job with your competitors, they are unlikely to have sufficiently detailed information or technical insight to make a major contribution. Competitive benchmarking tells you where you are and where they are but not how they got there.

However, real benefits can be produced because such comparisons almost always throw up key areas of difference, based purely on the ratios. Typical differentials could be profits before tax, employee productivity, gross margin, cash flow, and debt. With industry knowledge it is often fairly easy to guess at how your competitors do it. For some it could be pay policy or recruitment methods. For others it could be customer service or delivery terms. Each of these processes has a cost attached and you need to decide whether the cost of adapting competitor processes will deliver the improvements you are seeking.

The problem with this 'me too' approach is that you will always be behind the market, as you are simply copying what has already been invented. There is no competitive advantage. Some business consultants say that the cost of experimenting with new processes often outweighs the actual benefit for the pioneering company and that there is a case for always being second into the market with a new idea, as most innovations are relatively easy to copy. Working smart, they argue, is better than working hard and risking all.

I would argue that all companies are unique in what they do and how they do it. Following the leader creates the illusion that you will always be safe, as long as you keep close to them. The trouble is that no one knows when the leader will make a mistake and you could find yourself being dragged down the wrong strategic path without the resources necessary to take a hit. Gathering together processes that work for you is the way forward, even when you are looking at competitors. IBM is just one example of a company that followed the wrong path at the wrong time, in choosing to produce large systems rather than small PCs. Many smaller competitors went out of business simply because they were unwilling to accept that the market leader might have, albeit temporarily, got it wrong.

3. functional (non-competitive) benchmarking

The next option is to look at companies that are not competitors but may employ similar processes to your own in one or several parts of their organisation. At first glance, they may be features that are well known from a consumer perception – the rapid cooking and delivery of fast food, the distribution coverage of the mail service, the quality of a Rolls Royce. On closer examination, they may use processes that only become apparent after some investigation. For example, cash distribution around the country to local banks, consumer holiday telephone booking systems, the setting of fares within a national rail network. Depending on the process within your business that you may be hoping to improve, you could be looking at several kinds of benchmarking partners in several different industries at the same time.

4. generic benchmarking

The final option is to examine Best In Class, in other words those companies that have a recognised, leading reputation for managing a process that you do, but not quite as well. The objective is to study the processes of non-competitive market leaders that are directly comparable with your own processes. Once a study has been made, any improvements to your processes can be implemented in the knowledge that they are likely to be more efficient than your existing systems. Within the current copious literature on benchmarking, ranging from books to professional articles to references in business magazines to videos, these four types of benchmarking have acquired different interpretations. Functional benchmarking is sometimes referred to as process benchmarking. Competitive benchmarking, for some commentators, can mean financial comparisons. In other situations it can mean customer expectation comparisons – delivering 'delight' in any given product or service.

define what you mean

Distinguishing between different definitions or interpretations of benchmarking is not splitting hairs for the sake of it. Because the use of the word benchmarking has not yet achieved common, unambiguous understanding, each user needs to be sure their personal concept communicates well with those whose jobs it will eventually be to carry out the initiative. Each definition – internal, competitive, functional or generic – will require a commitment of resources and expertise to varying degrees. It is better to define what you mean at an early stage, otherwise what is seen by one manager as the beginning of the quest for the holy grail of market-leading quality could be wrongly interpreted by another manager as a quick fix for a manufacturing problem. But let us not get hung up on technicalities. In the words of Robert C Camp (1995), 'Benchmarking is simply the most efficient way to assure the success of a business change initiative.'

In summary, starting down the road to successful benchmarking means asking yourself and your fellow managers some pretty fundamental questions:

- ▓ What's wrong with what we do?
- ▓ How can we do it better?
- ▓ Will it gives us a competitive edge?
- ▓ Will our workforce be able to change?
- ▓ How much will it cost?

With these and other questions uppermost in your mind there is still one more critical question to find the answer to. Why benchmark at all? As the internal champion of benchmarking for your business, you need to have some good reasons to convince your colleagues and the staff that it is worth the inevitable upheaval in organisational terms to go down the benchmarking route.

why set benchmarks?

'Drill for oil? You mean drill into the ground to try and find oil? You're crazy.' Drillers protesting to Edwin L Drake when told about his project to drill for oil, 1859.
'Aeroplanes are interesting toys but of no military value.' Maréchal Foch, Professor of Strategy, Ecole Superieure de Guerre, 1921.
'Who the hell wants to hear actors talk.' H M Warner, Warner Bros, 1927.

Business is littered with anecdotal stories of breakthrough discoveries that set a new path for future profits. But few commentators quote the times when even the most eminent experts got it wrong.

If Tom Peters is right and the strategic aim of every company, large or small, is to survive, then examining the efficiency of those internal processes that help it survive (and flourish) should be a key corporate task. But how can benchmarking provide that framework? What special features of benchmarking guarantee that your company continues to get better as the months and years go by? Doesn't every company review its competitive performance all the time? They do when they compare historical financial performance but such analysis does not in any way point out how you can ensure the future success of your company.

reasons to benchmark

1. establishing the difference

The most important feature is the constant, systematic examination of what, in your customers' eyes, makes them buy from you, rather than your competitors. Benchmarking enables you to establish an internal standard for a product or service so that you can compare it with the marketplace, quickly and efficiently. The initial statement of product differential may well have been framed through market research, but only benchmarking provides the catalyst to examine the processes that contribute to giving your product its market differential.

2. setting the highest possible standards

Few people at work deliberately set out to produce poor service or shoddy goods. Most people would like to improve their work, if the resources and market allow. By knowing about the best processes in the world from many industries, there is a continuous opportunity through benchmarking to be able to set quality standards at the level of the very best and so aim for close to leading-edge results. You do not need to be the biggest company in size to produce the best quality products. Neither do you need to be the cheapest. Indeed in some markets price is less of an issue than a reliable and consistent quality of product.

3. learning from Best In Class (BIC)

Through benchmarking clubs and associations as well as site visits you can quickly assess whether a process in another industry could have applications for your company, with minimal cost or resource. The benchmarking ethic enables you to consider the tried and tested processes within organisations from around the world and apply them on a test basis, to minimise risk and investment. You may even be able to call on the BIC company for hands-on help in the early stages, if your benchmarking relationship is good enough.

4. creating synergy of ideas

Benchmarking does not simply mean the slavish copying of other people's ideas. The benchmarking implementation process involves comparing what others do well in conjunction with your own personnel and existing processes to see what borrowed elements will produce the desired improvement. Sometimes the entire process could replace an existing process. On other occasions, it may only be an approach, an outline concept or an adaptation. Whatever the degree of sharing, your company is more likely to benefit than be disadvantaged through benchmarking.

functional examples

When we consider the above reasons on a more practical level, the real benefits become more obvious. Take personnel policy, for example. You could start by examining whether recruitment policies are efficient throughout the organisation, not just at Head Office. You might consider standardising the current remuneration offer for managers across the business. You could even consider whether the training resources within the organisation are being used effectively. Is the information about why leavers leave being disseminated to everyone who needs to know?

One of the most fertile areas for savings are the administrative functions of the business, such as accounting. Is the department sufficiently computerised to make best use of human resources on the payroll? Could some tasks be undertaken by outside agencies more cheaply and efficiently? Perhaps a subsidiary has a particular skill/piece of software that could also be used in other parts of the business?

Manufacturing is often the best place to start, as there will be a number of mechanical processes that are easily measurable and can be compared with other areas of the business undertaking similar tasks. Stock inventories, delivery procedures, documentation errors, unavoidable downtime, absenteeism? Even if you run a service business, the same rules apply. Are customers in different divisions being serviced equally well? Are the billing procedures the most efficient way to chase debts? What research into consumer behaviour could be relevant right across the business rather than being kept for the consideration of one section only? Is there a company-wide preferred supplier list and if so, does everyone know who is on it?

But whether you are examining internal procedures or somebody else's, the task you will be engaged in is focusing on performance, with a view to setting a standard for the future.

focus on performance

The most famous example of the need for benchmarking comes from Robert C Camp, the founding father and leading guru on benchmarking techniques.

Robert C Camp: benchmarking pioneer

It was in the mid-1980s that Bob Camp a quality manager for Xerox Corporation, USA, first realised that the dwindling of Xerox Corporation's near monopoly on photocopier sales could be halted by examining the internal processes the organisation went through to provide the product to the consumer.

All aspects of this complex mix of processes were examined; price, service quality, manufacturing, marketing, distribution. Within the distribution process, Xerox Corporation compared their operational methods with 3M in Dusseldorf, Ford in Cologne, Sainsbury's regional depot in Hertfordshire, Volvo Parts in Gothenburg, and IBM. By comparing their own internal processes with the behaviour of perceived BIC companies, Xerox Corporation identified some major differences.

1. An extra stocking echelon that increased delivery turn-rounds and created extra cost.
2. Slower information flow.
3. No logistics representative at board level.
4. 'First Pick' availability of 83 per cent rather than the 90 per cent enjoyed by the companies studied.

This critical and regular approach to the examination of all Xerox Corporation's internal processes and the resulting improvements created a 40 per cent increase in customer satisfaction over four years (1987–91) and the creation of a world-wide managerial mind-set that says no process is sacred. Everything can be improved and should be improved on a regular basis.

During the course of this process Xerox discovered a number of important benefits as side-products of the benchmarking process:

- ▓ it promotes an attitude among the management and workforce that encourages innovation and positive criticism;
- ▓ it can increase awareness of the actual costs of certain processes;
- ▓ it encourages teamwork by involving work groups in the best management of their own tasks, so as to find the most efficient way.

In the final stages of Xerox's first foray into competitive benchmarking, they were awarded the prestigious Malcolm Baldridge National Quality Award (MBNQA) and they went on to win the European Quality Award in 1992. Gains in overall quality were a 78 per cent reduction in product defects, a 40 per cent decrease in unscheduled maintenance and a 27 per cent improvement in service response times.

However, the die-hards in your company may point out that all processes are improved all the time and that there is no real need to waste valuable resources looking for answers outside the confines of the plant or offices. In particular, some manufacturing management teams may consider any attempt to impose change as a threat to their own competence. You need to win the benchmarking argument using specific examples of quantifiable benefit. Concrete examples of higher efficiency through benchmarking will be your most powerful tool in establishing the need to act.

Many benchmarking projects can be justified on a pure cost-saving basis, without even having to take the high moral ground.

1. prevention costs

Better training, more efficient administrative controls and shorter delivery times means less waste and higher productivity. Taking action before minor inefficiencies become major cost problems is what benchmarking offers.

2. appraisal costs

More meaningful quality inspections, more critical internal audits and critical supplier usage provide managers with more time to manage personnel and less need to correct anomalies and change suppliers.

3. failure costs

Missed deliveries, mis-timed marketing, incorrect picking, inaccurate data, all have a cost as errors invariably need to be put right, taking up valuable resource and damaging existing customer relationships.

But more specific examples work best to win the argument for introducing benchmarking.

successful users of benchmarking techniques

- Procter & Gamble use a seven-point survey to monitor the effectiveness of their trade customer relationships. Over time this has resulted in loyal customers offering competitor information free on a regular basis, helping P&G to know quickly the marketing activity of their competitors.
- ICL benchmarks 20 of its competitors for overall financial performance and product technology. Distribution of comparative information is widespread within the company so that potential improvements can be identified at all levels of the organisation.
- Federal Express, the air cargo company, recorded a perfect score for its air cargo service within the USA from 53 per cent of its customers, following the introduction of TQM principles into the organisation. Its

nearest rival could only manage perfect scores from just 39 per cent. Since 1987 they have been recognised for their outstanding approach to quality issues, with no fewer than 195 awards.

▓ The Ritz-Carlton Hotel Company undertook to question customers about what processes were important to 'delight' guests. Nineteen separate processes were identified and then systematically improved and tested within hotel properties throughout the world. Specific goals were set (50 per cent cycle time reduction, 100 per cent guest retention) and a number of major service innovations were identified and standardised for the benefit of future guests.

▓ Texas Instruments in Sherman, Texas, identified $12,000 a month in operational expense savings and recouped its $54,000 capital and training investment by applying benchmarking techniques to the problem of rancid and unpleasant fluid odours on the shop floor.

Further testimony for benchmarking comes from a major study into productivity carried out in the United States by the Massachusetts Institute of Technology, which concluded: 'A characteristic of all the best-practice American firms we observed, large or small, is an emphasis on competitive benchmarking: comparing the performance of their products and processes with those of world leaders in order to achieve improvement and to measure progress'.

the Bradford Study

More proof of the effectiveness of benchmarking techniques comes from Professor Mohamed Zairi at the University of Bradford Management Centre. Twenty-nine companies known to be using extensive TQM techniques were measured over a five-year period to see whether the new techniques made any difference to the bottom line. Using eight common statistical ratios, such as profit per employee, return on total assets and profit margin, the Bradford Study showed that around 80 per cent of the companies studied were trading at above-average levels for their sector, the only differential being their usage of benchmarking techniques.

a final argument

The speed of technological advancement in the industrialised world has never been greater. Access to information has never been more widespread and with the growth of the Internet, it could be argued that the privileged power that knowledge has given in the past can no longer be sustained. Development times for many products and services have become remarkably short and in some markets, products could be obsolete within a few weeks of being launched.

As a result, companies can no longer afford to be inward-looking and rely on their own collective, intellectual resource to survive. They must look outside and gather best practice from other companies if they are to remain competitive in a global market.

Benchmarking provides the behaviour model within every organisation for the acceptance of rapid change and continuous improvement as a way of life, not just as something unusual to help cope with difficult market conditions.

Best Practice Benchmarking (BPB) has become a necessity for some of the world's largest corporations in their bid to retain their competitive edge. Your task is to use BPB in your own company to maintain and improve your market position by a regular, systematic and critical analysis of your company's internal processes.

what to benchmark?

If you have won the internal debate and the decision to benchmark has been given, half the battle has already been won. But the next stage can prove even tougher. Where to start?

It has been estimated, according to the UK Department of Trade and Industry, that 40 per cent of any benchmarking project resource is spent on the collection of data. It will therefore come as no surprise to realise that there is some way to go from the day you decide to benchmark to reaping the improved process benefits. The issue to confront is what to benchmark first.

Here is a typical list of potential internal processes requiring the benchmarking approach. At first glance, all could be equally important, depending your point of view.

possible processes to be benchmarked

Customer satisfaction	Correct invoicing
Cash management	Speed of service
Reducing set-up time	Innovation
Improving training	Pricing and purchasing
On-time delivery	Raw materials handling
Product consistency	Contract management

It is clear from the above list that improvements in some or all of these areas would make a difference to your company's bottom line. But you need to ask yourself which ones are critical to your business, particularly in the eyes of your customer.

Pure 'survival' factors such as operating within the law, paying your bills, and providing adequate employee health and safety are not good candidates for benchmarking. These are all activities you should be carrying out anyway. You need to identify the processes without which your business becomes uncompetitive.

Returning to the overriding philosophy of benchmarking, the question to ask is what you need to do to be better in your field of activity. It is likely that it will be a number of processes, which may or may not be connected, within the company, but which together create competitive performance.

a critical process

Within the printing industry, one element critical to success, in the customer's eyes, is after-sales service. Using customer research and a best practice club, PICON (an agency that represents suppliers to the printing, publishing, pulp, paper-making and converting industries) benchmarks the effectiveness of service from participating suppliers to their customers and so provides everyone in the club with the opportunity to alter their performance to everyone's advantage on a regular basis.

The Semiconductor Business Association (SBA) carries out a benchmarking programme on behalf of its specialist manufacturer members on the number of design iterations for integrated circuits. The higher the number the longer the delay in development for customers, and the lower the profitability.

In both these examples, benchmarking has been focused on what is critical for success in the relevant industries on the basis that resources are always scarce. Fix what is critical first.

the step zero concept

In a small company, what is critical to the business may be obvious. Deciding on which process to tackle first may simply be a question of calling a meeting and agreeing that there is a problem to be solved.

However, as organisations grow they become more complex and interdependency between working units can often confuse the overriding business priority. For that reason, most benchmarking companies set up a scoring system to determine which processes to improve first. Robert C Camp's view is that before getting our hands dirty in scoring processes, we should go back one step – to step zero – and ask ourselves who the eventual internal customer is for a process. By identifying the output of a process study (the result of the process change) and the internal customer you can validate and give credibility to your benchmarking focus. For example, if a process you have initially identified has no internal customer (quite literally, nobody in the organisation is keen to buy the improved process) it should not be benchmarked. It is the customer who should commission the team and see the urgent need for change. The communication of the work schedule should also be laid out so that the customer, your internal sponsor, is completely aware of what will be required. As Robert C Camp says, 'The purpose of step zero is to obtain consensus on the key facets of the benchmarking investigation before it is launched.' Benchmarking is not something that can be imposed on an unwilling business unit by a remote administration team.

ranking your processes

So, assuming you have some willing and enthusiastic internal customers, you now need to score your process candidates for benchmarking so that scarce resources can be focused on critical areas. It is particularly important if your company is new to benchmarking that you produce quantifiable results, so that internal confidence in the technique grows. Scoring possible processes is therefore a logical way to make the selection, just to double-check that you are investigating the right parts of the organisation.

Some businesses start by looking at every single process, in order to arrive at those that appear to be the most important. This is without doubt the most rigorous but also the most time-consuming approach to benchmarking. Taking an overall view of the whole organisation could take years if it is your intention to leave no stone unturned. A more practical approach for most businesses is to list the processes that have a critical direct influence in two areas:

1. Customer expectations.
2. Bottom-line profitability.

Under these two headings, most managers familiar with the business could quite easily draw up a shortlist of areas for improvement. For example:

Customer Expectations	Bottom Line Profitability
Market planning	Financial planning
Customer support	Physical asset acquisition
Order processing	Information technology
Delivery	Management systems
Production/manufacturing	Accounting operations
Service territory planning	Pricing
Logistics	Invoicing
Hiring and assignment	Collection
Research and development	Leasing

The list is a reflection of a particular type of company in a particular kind of market. Each shortlist will be different depending on the circumstances of the company. It can be argued that every company needs to look at every process however indirect. But in the first instance, getting going with benchmarking is more important than getting it perfect.

Once the lists have been drawn up, the challenge now is to rank them in order of priority.

ranking for priority

Depending on which function you work in, you will have a different view as to what needs to be done first. For the sales director wanting to get sales territory planning right, using efficient software could save a lot of internal debate between salesmen regarding commissions and credit. For the production director, a thorough reappraisal of the picking system in the warehouse for raw materials could, he is convinced, deliver much-reduced lead times, which he knows would be warmly welcomed by all. Meanwhile, the financial director is adamant that the introduction of a new cost-accounting system would immediately translate into profits. Vested interests will always play a part at this stage, as some managers may feel that they should strike while the iron is hot and resources appear to be on the table. Lobbying to get a particular project initiated is common, once a potential list has been published in management papers.

What is needed is a sensible way to choose what to do and in what order. Many organisations use a combination of outside consultants, their auditors and a specific team of internal managers to debate the priority list. But the more successful decisions include reference to which areas could be *most improved* and which areas could *impact the bottom line* directly. Each process could be costed and given a high, medium or low rating against its bottom-line impact. Similarly, you could rate the potential for improvement along similar lines. Another moderating factor could be whether the process in question needs to be done now, soon or some time in the future. By drawing up a table with these factors side by side, candidates for immediate action soon become clear, but with the aim to tackle the other processes in due course as part of an overall plan.

You can clearly go much deeper into the deciding factors. Often, organisations use the basic elements of their strategic plan to help them decide for or against each process-improvement candidate. Questions such as whether the process would contribute to customer satisfaction, whether it would have critical future potential for development, and whether it would cost a lot to implement could well be useful to help you decide between seemingly equally deserving cases.

Consultancies that specialise in benchmarking have a ready-made list of potential processes for improvement as part of their stock-in-trade which can be used an aide-memoire if you think you need to go back to basics or even be reminded of something you had not even considered. This prioritisation method is sometimes called the Analytical Hierarchy Process, or AHP for short.

Analytical Hierarchy Process

The AHP is not as complex as it sounds. It simply provides a framework for scoring relative importance without the emotional involvement of sponsoring (or lukewarm) departmental managers.

The approach involves rating the process against a maximum weighted score, previously determined. Typical criteria could be importance to the organisation (perceived criticality), current perceived skill, time needed to complete the analysis, availability of resources, willingness of the customer to participate, as well as the other factors mentioned above.

Using a score of 100, and weighting each factor, you can arrive at a rating, so that other processes can be directly compared. Depending on your market circumstances, you may consider 'urgency need' to be a factor, which could change your view of where to start your benchmarking initiative.

If you consider that most companies can identify anywhere between 80–160 key work processes and that around 15 per cent or so could be improved at any one time, the documentation alone would keep the entire Human Resources team busy full time.

Whatever pecking order the ranking procedure reveals, always temper the decision with management consensus. Benchmarking against the flow is unlikely to produce sound results.

be critical: things change

Much satisfaction will be gained from the establishment of the priority list. Even more self-congratulation may be appropriate once work on the mapping of processes begins, but a word of caution. One of the principles of the benchmarking ethic is to be critical of current processes on a regular basis. This should extend to the benchmarking process itself. At any moment, the process you had not intended to benchmark could become more critical. In an industry where the supply of raw materials appears infinite, (oil, water, gas), examining how such raw materials are supplied may appear less critical if all your competitors are governed by the same acquisition process.

But what if things change? What if, for political, geographical or economic reasons, the raw materials were no longer available to your company on an equal footing? Suddenly the supply of raw materials would come to the top of the critical processes list and others ranked towards the bottom might have to be dropped.

The reverse is also true. Processes that on first investigation appear to be top priorities could turn out to be market-leading processes themselves, and as such need less development than other, more worthy, problem areas.

The task is to review the processes being worked on regularly so that your resources are used to the optimum. Benchmarking too many processes is as equally unwelcome as benchmarking too few.

the importance of management commitment

Benchmarking often requires a new way of looking at your organisation. For some managers it may also be a time when they feel, for whatever reason, under pressure to perform. After all, if one of their departmental processes emerges as one of the areas for action in the first phase, they may feel guilty that they did not spot the problem themselves and may be unwilling to lend cooperation to the change team. Management commitment is vital in the 'no blame' culture of performance improvement.

Studies in the United States have shown a predictable and consistently similar rank order of reasons why some TQM/benchmarking initiatives fail. Top of the list is senior and middle management commitment, followed by a lack of focus concerning customer satisfaction and the organisation's mission statement. There is further evidence that poor internal communication of the benefits is also a critical factor for failure. It is clearly vital, therefore, that once the list for action has been drawn up a clear and consistent effort is made to get senior management on board, so that any new initiatives can be carried out effectively. Benchmarking as a way of corporate life then becomes a strategic issue rather than simply another internal project that may attract varying degrees of internal follow-through.

mapping your processes

Now you are aware of what kind of processes should be benchmarked, the next task is to map them. It is quite likely that no one has attempted to examine your company before in quite this way, so some patience will be needed to get this next stage right. It will almost certainly require you to develop a deeper understanding of what people actually do within their business unit as opposed to what they say they do or what you may think they do. Depending on your own business experience, you may even learn something at the same time.

This stage of benchmarking is known as mapping the processes. In short, what you produce will be a series of diagrammatic descriptions of your key processes, so that you can examine them for efficiency and compare them with processes in other businesses or with themselves or other processes within your own business when you have implemented future improvements.

the helicopter view

Every business can be rationalised into simple steps if you take an overall or helicopter view. All successful businesses tend to follow a similar pattern, as indicated in Figure 4.1

What makes one business more successful than another is the detailed way each element of the cycle is organised. We have already agreed that to map the processes of an entire organisation could take a long time. Most businesses have more than 80 separate processes which, when interacting, make that business unique. But that is no reason to flinch from the task of trying to isolate some of those processes.

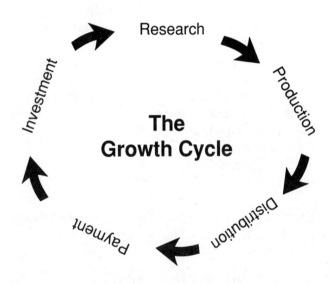

Figure 4.1 *The growth cycle*

Equally, those involved in the day-to-day running of the business can see the obvious candidates for operational improvement. The classic compromise is the best solution. You should attempt to do both because, by acknowledging all your processes while progressing with the detailed mapping of acknowledged critical processes, you will be achieving the short- and long-term aims of the new benchmarking culture.

techniques for processes

Depending on your commercial background, you will feel naturally more comfortable with one analytical technique rather than another. However, using techniques that may be outside your normal experience can reveal insights into parts of the business that perhaps you never really understood. Laying bare the essentials of every process is what is required, if the eventual benchmarking is to be robust.

Here are some process identification techniques:

1. Performance and practices.
2. Flowcharting.
3. Arrow/mind map.
4. Cause and effect.
5. Supply chain.
6. Matrix.

These techniques can be applied both to the whole organisation or parts of the whole, to equal effect.

check the big picture first

Often, the root cause of corporate inefficiency can be laid at the door of functional organisation. This is particularly true of fast-growing companies that have never found the time to examine themselves critically using standard benchmarks of departmental performance. It is therefore a good idea not to assume that you are organised in the most efficient way at the top level. At the most basic level, Figure 4.2 shows how efficient companies should be organised:

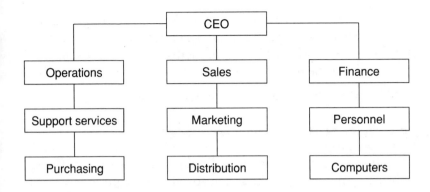

Figure 4.2 *Typical functional organogram*

As organisations grow, more functions are added but not always in a logical sequence. It is common for some new divisions to be headed by the finance director, if only to keep an eye on costs. A few years down the line the company finds that such a division still reports to the board through that channel, whether or not it is still appropriate.

One of the drawbacks of this type of hierarchy is the implication that the higher up you are, the more you know. The reverse is often a more accurate statement. It may be more efficient to have more functional heads working as a management advisory group, allowing the board of three or four directors to consider purely strategic and long-term investment issues.

Equally, too many managers and supervisors can create inefficiencies of their own. We all know about work expanding to fit the time available, but virtually everyone in medium-to-large enterprises has seen an increase in the number of managers who simply monitor performance rather than add to the process. Whenever there is a downturn in the economy, these levels of non-productive supervisors are often the first ones to be downsized, because financial analysis shows that they not only slow the production down, but also represent a

cost with no added value. So be critical of current organisational structures before you start specific process analysis. You
may be able to solve a number of inefficient practices simply by
reorganising the top or middle management team, unpalatable
as that may be.

performance and practices

You may have initially identified eight or nine key areas of your
business that you think, if improved, could provide critical
competitiveness. Simply build a tree diagram that links desired
performance to the process involved.

Imagine a tree turned on its side with foliage to the left and
roots to the right. The branches on the left represent key
processes in the business. The roots to the right represent
specific elements in each process.

Each element could then have additional 'subroots'
depending on the complexity of the process. Such a diagram
would provide a detailed overview of the processes and
elements under discussion (see Figure 4.3).

flowcharting

This is a common technique in systems programming with its
own symbolic language, designed to communicate sequential
steps in the most efficient way. Because benchmarking
processes can be analysed in a similar manner, flowcharting is a
popular technique.

Some common flowcharting symbols can be seen in Figure
4.4.

You may wish to add your own symbols to personalise
certain elements peculiar to your business. By building a flow
diagram with a vertical line (the symbols are at the top hori-
zontally), you can, at a glance, see what parts of the operation
dominate any particular process. You can then critically

examine those elements of the process for potential further study or even compare them visually with flowcharts of similar processes in other businesses.

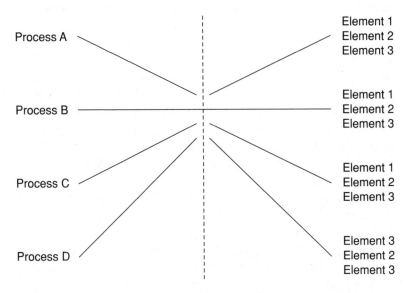

Figure 4.3 *Tree diagram*

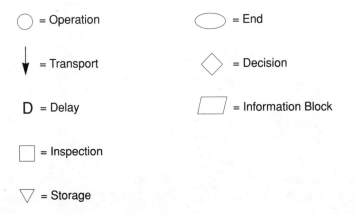

Figure 4.4 *Flowcharting symbols*

In an ideal world a flowchart should show how the input becomes the output in a straight line over the shortest possible time. In the simple example shown in Figure 4.5, you can see immediately that there is a delay in the process as represented by steps 3 and 4. This is the part of the process that would require investigation as to why this is so. There may be a very good reason, perhaps to do with suppliers or some kind of inspection. But once identified it should make you consider how to improve the situation. The diagram may also show a gap. For example, in Figure 4.5 the operation appears to go from inspection to finish. However, it is likely that the product will be taken to a warehouse and stored. By drawing up a flow-chart you can quickly identify inaccuracies and/or errors and act accordingly.

It is important to be aware of bias when compiling such flowcharts. The departments involved will be naturally suspi-cious of the organisation's intentions when the results are published, so it is not advisable to simply give the task to the department head to complete. There may be a part of the process that he or she enjoys supervising personally, such as inspection or supplier negotiation, and would be reluctant to give up, in which case it might be omitted from the official

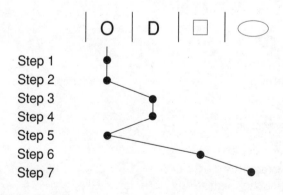

Figure 4.5 *Process flowchart*

flowchart. Another factor to consider is that managers who are close to a process tend to become blinkered to its potential absurdities and fail to question the reasons why certain parts of the operational cycle are the way they are. It needs an objective outsider to ask the apparently silly questions.

When the operational flowcharts have been completed correctly you should be faced with a number of areas for improvement. Typical findings include bulky reports with no obvious use, inadequate delegation of tasks, uneven workflow, duplication of tasks, too many inspections, unsuitable performance figures, lack of links to the financial function, and no written instructions for the process. At the very least a flowchart analysis should give the supervisory team, perhaps for the first time, an easy-to-understand description of what they actually do, so that they can start to think how to do it better in future.

arrow diagrams (mind mapping)

Arrow diagrams (see Figure 4.6) are a variation of flowcharting that allow you to create an overview of the inter-relationships between elements of the process in a less linear format.

Typically, arrow diagrams present a series of decision trees that lead to different end results. Such diagrams are particularly useful when analysing interaction between departments and will quickly highlight any organisational anomalies (eg why does accounts organise the sales conference?).

Mind-mapping is an extension of an arrows diagram and a useful technique when gathering ideas from a group of people, all of whom may need to contribute in order to get an accurate map of the process. It also highlights how the activities of departments somewhat removed from the process under examination may be revealed to be crucial to its efficient operation although not directly involved in any output.

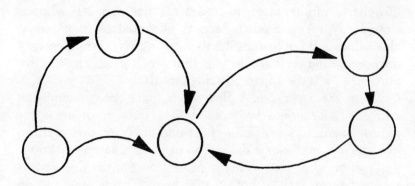

Figure 4.6 *An arrow diagram*

This technique is also beneficial when it comes to brain-storming new ideas for improvement, as the best ideas often come from those who have only a partial link to the process under review.

cause and effect

Another way to identify the separate elements of a process is to draw a line in a time sequence (one hour, day or month, or whatever), with herringbone lines above and below to delineate influences on the overall process as the operation progresses. Variously referred to as fishbones, Godzilla's bones or Ishikawa, cause and effect diagrams (see Figure 4.7) help to clarify interdepartmental or inter-organised links where they may not be obvious at first glance.

Kaoru Ishikawa is a leading practitioner of TQM in Japan and was the first to put into practice quality-control circles. His fishbone diagrams are characterised by the underlying timeline that is the measure of the efficiency of the process. Any deals will result in a less-efficient result. Coupled with the extensive use of statistical analysis, Ishikawa has shown that over 95 per

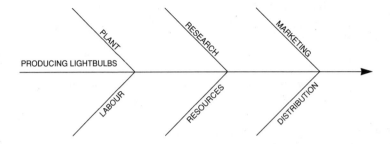

Figure 4.7 *A cause and effect diagram*

cent of all process problems can be solved using statistics and that this form of continuous measurement should not just be left to official inspectors. All workers in the process should be able to monitor the efficiency of the process and adjust their own behaviour accordingly.

supply chain

You could describe each process as a series of links in a chain, sometimes with a beginning and an end, sometimes circular. The supply-chain method helps you to highlight interdependency of essential elements within the chain. Such analysis can assist organisations in assessing whether they should create, where possible, their own alternative supply link in the event that the existing relationships with organisations in the chain become untenable or uneconomic.

matrix

Many processes have vertical and horizontal components. Matrices can help clarify a pattern so that the differences in volume highlight a specific reason for that difference.

For example when comparing two manufacturing processes,

a simple matrix for each business unit could reveal overman-
ning in a certain area, which would lead you to investigate in
more detail.

	Distribution	Paintshop	Finishing	Warehouse	Efficiency index
Company A	5	10	6	2	75
Company B	3	2	6	1	100
Company C	4	2	5	7	55

Without knowing the facts, it would appear from this matrix
that Company C has far too many people in the warehouse and
so warrants further investigation as to why. Equally, Company
A has too many people in the paintshop.

The benchmarker's task would be to clarify the key processes
of all three companies and suggest what best practice could be
followed to achieve greater efficiency.

which mapping techniques should you use?

There is no hard and fast rule about process identification and
mapping. Some internal audiences are more used to seeing
operations represented diagrammatically. Others need a
sequential story. Others still may want it written out, memo-
style.

The overriding objective is to get to the heart of a key
process, but then seek management or operational consensus
that the process map is an accurate description of what actually
happens in practice. Once this part of benchmarking is
complete you will have identified how your business units go
about particular tasks.

Deficiencies will become apparent in some areas because the act of examination will undoubtedly bring into question the established way of doing things. However, other elements may not be so obvious. Is seven days good or bad as the average turnaround time for a sales promotion campaign from a leading agency? Is a parts stock availability of 85 per cent for a major automotive manufacturer adequate? Should you be disappointed if 20 per cent of all the life insurance your sales-force sells in a year does not stay on the books the following year? Above all, have you gathered the data in a consistent way so that you can be categoric about performance levels when it comes to comparing your performance with the performance of other organisations?

gathering the benchmark data

Now you have chosen the processes to be benchmarked and mapped your critical processes, you need to establish a system for gathering relevant data. The laborious but rewarding task of process mapping has had but one aim – to establish robust performance measures for future comparison. But too much of the wrong type of data could render the entire initiative ineffective. Gathering and presenting consistent data is the key to successful benchmarking.

Each process, once analysed, will produce a quantifiable result. Some will be hard measures (productivity, ratios, time), others will be softer measures (reputation, attitude, innovation) but no less worthy because they are soft.

One cautionary note is to ensure that the measurement you are using is logical and consistent with the way other companies measure their own performance, otherwise comparisons will become meaningless.

At its simplest level, for example, measuring profit should be before tax, not after tax, as taxation treatment varies from business to business and from country to country. Similarly, number of employees should be those in full-time employment, unless the nature of your business is such that the part-time workforce plays a significant part in your overall efficiency or the performance of your industry sector.

the data collection plan

According to UK Department of Trade and Industry figures a significant proportion of the resources allocated to benchmarking projects is spent on data collection. It therefore makes sense to plan the process in the same way that any other process is planned for maximum efficiency. There will be inputs (sources) and outputs (results or performance indicators).

Sources will be both internal and external, but depending on which of the four types of benchmarking being undertaken (see Chapter 1) there will be a variety of collection methods.

internal benchmarking

It is likely that in your analysis of internal processes you will come across many data sources of differing quality. Few businesses develop to the level of profitability without producing some basic statistical information.

The managers and operatives in the various departments under scrutiny will have both a formal and an informal list of how they measure the performance of their processes.

At the managerial level, it is likely that the departmental or senior expert in the process will have a clear idea of what measures over time are more meaningful than others. It is well worth listening carefully to what the specialist says, although be mindful that habit does play a part in self-regulation.

It could be that the overall measurement in the workplace has been speed of operation. If this is how successive managers have been assessed by their superiors in the hierarchy, more important elements such as quality (product consistency) could have been overlooked. As the champion of benchmarking in your organisation, you are allowed to be professionally critical about past and current assessments of what constitutes successful performance.

internal data

When you are collecting internal data you need to be aware of the two uses to which it will be put. The first is to help you set standards of operational efficiency within the company. The second is to have data available for external comparison at some future date. It is also worth remembering that the data has to be meaningful, as the cost of collection may be a significant factor in whether you ever get round to implementing what you have recognised as best practice. Typical 'hard' lists from internal sources could include:

- cost per item;
- productivity;
- stock level;
- staffing level;
- achievement of deadlines;
- spoiled goods;
- customer returns;
- materials used;
- back orders;
- cash flow;
- late payments.

Depending on the complexity of your business, this list could be much longer and more detailed, but only collect data that has a purpose.

Benchmarking also includes 'soft' items, which could be equally important in a competitive situation, so you need to consider what soft information you want to gather, though it is

likely you will have fewer soft items than hard ones. A typical
list of soft items could include:

- range of products;
- after-sales costs;
- direct delivery to customers;
- customer-perceived satisfaction;
- repeat business;
- positive comments from customers;
- accuracy of sales forecasts;
- product enhancements;
- industry reputation among peers;
- exit interviews from leavers.

Another aspect of information to gather is what characterises a
company in terms of behaviour or general market performance. Each organisation has a unique blend of attributes,
which sometimes work in its favour, sometimes not. These
prevailing attitudes shape corporate policy on a very subtle
level and should be logged as data for benchmarking purposes.
A business with a reputation for fair dealing and quality may
be underperforming because its accounts department is too
aggressive in its debt-collection policy. By establishing the
industry norm and doing a comparison, the improvement
could be to be less aggressive on debt and more careful which
clients to deal with in the first place.

competitive benchmarking

Collecting data for external comparison needs planning and
constant vigilance for consistency. Within the financial arena,
the legal conventions of accountancy enable you to compare
like for like in a relatively straightforward way.

Typical measures would be turnover, profit before tax, return
on capital employed, productivity per employee, growth,
margin, investment. However, take care if you use informal

industry surveys, such as those computed by trade magazines to boost circulation. You may need to look carefully at how the statistics were compiled. Often, major market players are missing for all kinds of reasons and less successful competitors tend to overstate their results to improve their PR standing.

The most reliable sources are regular reports compiled by industry associations, taken from audited accounts, whose member companies subscribe on an annual basis so that they can compare statistical performance.

The Society of Motor Manufacturers and Traders (SMMT) in the UK provides for the automotive industry a comprehensive breakdown of unit sales of cars sold over specific periods, thereby providing a swift and reliable measurement of market share.

However, in less mature industries, such as computers or mobile telephones, statistics become less reliable, so indications can only be taken from reports based on consumer sales or from companies' figures submitted on a voluntary basis.

Professional associations for functions (Institute of Directors, Industrial Society, Institute of Marketing) can be a good source of reliable information about best practice when examining processes, although because the data is sporadic they can only serve as indicators of general trends or specific techniques.

As for your customers, not only can they provide ongoing ratings for your own performance, but they are a good source of competitive information. However, once again, be critical about the 'halo' effect of what your customers say to you and why. Often, praise about your competitors could be simply a negotiating ploy to encourage you to shave your margins or provide a disproportionately higher level of service.

Examining why customers say what they do, rather than accepting it as fact, is an essential part of information gathering and best handled by a research agency who, through statistical cross-checks and balances, can sort the truth from the untruths.

Collecting competitive data is a creative task rather than

purely analytical. It can demand a degree of detective work to find the right sources. Make sure you exhaust all the avenues available before deciding on the most reliable measures of competitive performance.

Some examples of competitive information sources

Business libraries	Syndicated research
Seminars	Professional associations
Industry experts	Your field- or sales-forces
Trade magazines	Academics
Customers	Electronic files
Suppliers	Stockbrokers
Annual reports	Industry watchdogs/
Government statistics	regulators

---

functional benchmarking data

Gathering data about non-competitors is easier in that if the right partners are chosen, bias can be eliminated. Functional benchmarking data comes from an exchange of information about particular business processes rather than, say, financial performance or market share.

How to go about finding the right benchmarking partners is dealt with in Chapter 6. A site visit to the premises of the partner can be a good way to gather relevant information but it is by means the only way and often this is the culmination of much pre-planning rather than the initial step. Everyone has a busy schedule and no benchmarking partner will remain courteous if you continually press for unprepared visits.

Telephone surveys of non-competitor companies known to employ similar processes can be an efficient way to gather relevant data. Written questionnaires can be useful for more complex processes but be prepared for less than 10 per cent response.

For those companies who share common technology, tele-conferencing or the Internet can provide an efficient way to exchange information without the need for time out of the office or time-consuming protocol.

Collecting functional non-competitor benchmarking data is more about working practices than performance as efficiencies in one industry may not be practical in another, non-competing industry. Mapping non-competitor processes could be the most valuable aspect of all benchmarking initiatives, so be prepared to ask why things are done the way they are and think how certain parts of the process could be adapted to your business. Wholesale copying of a non-competitor's processes is unlikely to produce real benefits. Creative adaptation is the key.

generic benchmarking data

Generic benchmarking is all about learning from Best In Class (BIC) companies. Thanks to such initiatives as the European Foundation for Quality Management (EFQM) and the Malcolm Baldridge National Quality Award (MBNQA) in the United States, there is now a lot of reliable information available about best benchmarking practice on a national and global basis.

For example, IFS International Ltd, based in Bedford, is a UK benchmarking clearing house that provides a forum for information through its Best Practice Club. A combination of printed material, seminars, video courses and newsletters helps the would-be benchmarking organisation not only learn the techniques but also gather relevant case history material.

The *Best Practice Magazine* contains regular features on how leading companies did things better. The magazine has included features on Motorola, Truprint, Richer Sound, Marriott Hotels, British Steel and Unipart, among many others.

Specific functional benchmarking clearing houses include the ICC Information Group for financial information, the Reward Group for personnel-related issues, as well as most of the major UK management consultancies, who often have specific expertise in particular industry sectors.

software and data

How you store the data you have gathered will be of crucial importance once the process performance standards have been set. It will also help you cover all the angles as you progress.

Storyboard-style software has been developed by some organisations so that the internal team and their eventual partners can see quickly the processes being discussed and can make 'live' changes as the understanding and discussions lengthen.

Data presentation in the form of bar charts, pie charts, straight-line conformances or graphs need to be developed so that comparisons can be made swiftly using the same data.

The technical aspects of the program are not complex, but as in most initiatives for action you will need to think about the presentation and the mathematical analysis while you are gathering the data. A database full of information is no good if it cannot be analysed and presented in a user-friendly format.

almost there

By this stage you will have mapped your most critical processes and have at your fingertips the relevant data collection procedures. You will have determined some universally comparable measures for your own internal performance across a series of processes and be aware of best practice performance among competitors and non-competitors, albeit through desk research.

The next step is what makes benchmarking such a creative technique for improvement: systematic on-site learning from other non-competitor companies. Finding the right benchmarking partners to visit will be one of the most important elements of the plan.

benchmarking partnerships with non-competitors

Companies new to benchmarking often assume that setting up benchmarking partnerships means choosing a single, non-competing organisation and establishing a formal link for ongoing comparison at many levels.

If this were the case, the technique of benchmarking would be comparatively simple and everyone would do it all the time. The practical truth is somewhat different. The true benchmarker will establish links with several partners in different industries, if the technique is being used correctly.

We have already established (see Chapter 3) that you may have a number of possibly unconnected processes that are critical to your business, which you would like to perform better. You will have also discovered that the easiest place to start benchmarking is within your own company. Taking these discoveries into account, your search for benchmarking partnership is most likely to take the following pattern.

compiling a list of partners

1. Business units within your own extended organisation or its non-competing subsidiaries.
2. Non-competing companies that seem to exhibit leading performance in one, some or many of your critical processes, in other industries.
3. Acknowledged national or global leaders in your critical processes.

All three of these routes have advantages and disadvantages. But before you book your business-class ticket to Japan, let us just consider for a moment the benchmarking partner that is going to be the most efficient for your organisation or division.

General criteria for choosing a benchmarking partner may include the overall size of the potential partner, reputation in the marketplace, the type of ownership, its organisational structure, its geography, and its distribution methods. This is on the basis that the company is unlikely to provide time and access to an outside organisation unless it is of a similar standing. The next step could be to consider whether you are looking to examine processes for possible adaptation or simply standard measures against which you can gauge your own performance for a particular process.

One of the key issues is to make the opportunity to benchmark as attractive for the other party as it is for you. Some thought needs to be given to how you can reciprocate once you have gathered the benefits through data collection and discussion.

Large companies like IBM, American Express and Xerox Corporation do extensive research long before they approach a potential partner. This research includes a formal process of sifting through data such as lists of quality-award winners, top-rated industry-sector firms, trade magazine articles, reports from financial advisers, supplier recommendations and open or closed surveys, to determine whether the potential partner will be able to deliver sufficiently useful processes. At the end of this drawing up of a shortlist, ratings will be given to each potential partner for each process under investigation and priorities will be assigned, depending on the urgency of the organisation's need to benchmark these processes. It is likely you will have several targets in mind at any one time because not every target will be willing to benchmark on request. They may already be committed to other benchmark partners or their current trading position may mean they would have to postpone a decision, as in the case of an imminent merger or stock market flotation.

business units within your own organisation

The most convenient route is to go local. If you remember that you are looking for best practice in the processes that you currently employ, it is highly likely that sister companies in the group or overseas subsidiaries owned by the group will be operating similar processes more efficiently; especially if their technology has over the years copied and improved the original company's technology.

Access to detailed information about how your sister company achieves its 'excellent record of productivity' could be obtained relatively easily, through the normal hierarchy of management. Exchange of data can be instant if the company operates an 'on-line' communication strategy. Specific queries about detail could be clarified with an informal telephone call or tele-conference. Rank Xerox did just that with Fuji Xerox, their Japanese subsidiary, to learn how to shorten their new product development cycle. If you are both manufacturing the same product, comparisons of efficiency can be made quickly and best practice adopted across the comparable parts of the organisation. However, there are two main stumbling blocks:

1. Internal politics.
2. Step-change dynamics.

internal politics

Most multinationals are highly competitive, even within the confines of the same corporation. Often, regions of the world compete for development resources from a central fund, so 'being the best' at the year-end is a useful bargaining tool for expanding operations in your part of the world.

It has to be said that not all members of the corporate family always strive for the common good. You may find that by choosing a business unit too close geographically or technologically to your own type of operation, petty jealousies can creep in and block your progress. The last thing you want is an internal political battle. So you may be better advised to look at similar business units outside your own division or part of the world.

step change dynamics

Human nature tells us that we are all creatures of habit, and business is no exception. By benchmarking your processes only with companies within the group, you are likely to make steady, but not spectacular, progress.

The power of peer group pressure is great and in shaving off comparatively small performance gains, you may miss the creative insight to make a truly radical step change that could catapult your company towards spectacular, step-change performance improvement.

non-competing companies

The most fruitful partnerships come from this second category. Their great advantage is that they offer the enthusiastic bench- marker the opportunity to examine completely different ways of managing processes, some of which may be truly innovative.

Drawing up a shortlist of such partners takes time and requires an element of creativity. Often the companies you are the closest to are your suppliers. If they are regular suppliers you probably already know their strengths as well as their weaknesses. If they are successful with you, it is highly likely there is some process they go through that is to be admired in their class, otherwise you would be doing business with their direct competitors. Most suppliers are only too willing to develop an already successful relationship in this way.

The next potential list of non-competing partners can come from information in the public domain. Professional informa- tion and research consultants are able to scour trade and busi- ness periodicals and come up with a shortlist of 'admirable' companies who may have something to offer in your search for best practice.

Associations are a reliable source of other likely candidates, although detail about specific processes will be lacking. Increasingly, benchmarking clearing houses can offer potential links through their databases for a relatively small sum. But you may find that attending seminars or networking events is a more efficient way to get down to the brass tacks of comparing similar processes and so short-circuit the initial approach and the inevitable protocol of formal meetings.

One point to bear in mind with non-competing partners is simply that of size. Large conglomerates have large resources. The reason why their process may work better than yours could be the support services available to get the right result. However admirable the process it may be that, for a small or even a medium-sized company, the resource required to improve that process in the manner suggested by the large conglomerate will be out of the question, financially speaking. So, you need to consider the resources available, if you hope to emulate a non-competitive process.

Best In Class

The luxury approach to benchmarking is to go for Best In Class. Such companies are acknowledged leaders in their markets, either absolutely or in a number of critical processes, which together create their market-leading position. A glance at the *Financial Times Actuaries 500 Share Index*, or in the USA, the *Fortune 500*, will tell you who they are. There will be many examples from these companies of best practice processes, which are widely disseminated in a variety of business magazines, complete with indexed data showing real improvements achieved.

However, the success of these companies can also limit their potential use as partners. Many of the world's top companies who have become acknowledged benchmarking practitioners are starting to charge for their time and for their data, in recognition of the resources such dissemination of information use up. Some even specify the size and type of non-competitor they would be prepared to share information with on an ongoing basis. To some extent they have become victims of their own benchmarking PR.

Clearly, to all of these list-building approaches you can add personal contacts, your own business knowledge, members of functional organisations or even a daily systematic trawling of the business press. The objective is to draw up a large list of potential partners for each process and then reduce that list to a shortlist that you are going to approach with a meaningful proposition.

code of conduct

There is one final piece of preparatory work you need to agree internally before progressing towards a likely benchmarking partner. You need to establish some ground rules for the exchange of information.

The Benchmarking Centre published some years ago a suggested code of conduct for all participating partners, which is reproduced below, with their kind permission.

the benchmarking code of conduct

To contribute to efficient, effective ethical benchmarking, individuals agree for themselves and their organisation to abide by the following principles for benchmarking with other organisations.

1. principle of legality
Avoid discussions or actions that might lead to or imply an interest in restraint of trade; market or customer allocation schemes; price fixing; dealing arrangements; bid rigging; bribery; or misappropriation. Do not discuss costs with competitors if costs are an element of pricing.

2. principle of exchange
Be willing to provide the same level of information that you request in any benchmarking exchange.

3. principle of confidentiality
Treat benchmarking interchange as something confidential to the individuals and organisations involved. Information obtained must not be communicated outside the partnering organisations without prior consent of participating benchmarking partners. An organisation's participation in a study should not be communicated externally without their permission.

4. principle of use
Use of information obtained through benchmarking partnering is only for the purpose of improvement of operations with the partnering companies themselves. External use of communication of a benchmarking partner's name with their data or observed practices requires permission of that partner. Do not, as a consultant or client, extend one company's benchmarking study findings to another without the first company's permission.

5. principles of first party contact
Initiate contacts, whenever possible, through a benchmarking contact designated by the partner company. Obtain mutual agreement with the contact on any handover of communication or responsibility to other parties.

6. principle of third party contact
Obtain an individual's permission before providing their name in response to a contact request.

7. principle of preparation
Demonstrate commitment to the efficiency and effectiveness of the benchmarking process with adequate preparation at each process step, particularly at initial partnering contact.

ETIQUETTE AND ETHICS

- In actions between benchmarking partners, the emphasis is on openness and trust. The following guidelines apply to both partners in a benchmarking encounter:
- In benchmarking with competitors, establish specific ground rules up front, eg 'We do not want to talk about those things that will give either of us a competitive advantage, rather, we want to see where we both can mutually improve or gain benefit.'
- Do not ask competitors for sensitive data or cause the benchmarking partner to feel that sensitive data must be provided to keep the process going.

- ▧ Use an ethical third party to assemble any blind competitive data, with inputs from legal counsel, for direct competitor comparisons.
- ▧ Consult with legal counsel if any information-gathering procedure is in doubt, eg before contacting a direct competitor.
- ▧ Any information obtained from a benchmarking partner should be treated as internal privileged information.

DO NOT

- ▧ Disparage a competitor's business or operations to a third party.
- ▧ Attempt to limit competition or gain business through the benchmarking relationship.

As you can see, some of the provisions are quite specific but merely underline the seriousness of the initiative you may be undertaking. You can assume the benchmarking partner is conversant with those ground rules so make sure your team is equally prepared and knowledgeable.

European Code of Benchmarking

There has been discussion in the past that exchanging confidential information such as in the benchmarking process contravenes Article 76 of the Treaty of Rome, which makes illegal the collusion of competitors to gain commercial advantage. Although benchmarking is a win–win situation for both parties, for the unaware it could be construed in some circumstances as industrial espionage. Competition law both in the European Union (EU) and other countries expressly forbids any collusion between direct competitors to gain an unfair market advantage.

The European Commission has the power to fine organisations up to 10 per cent of their annual turnover for breach of competition law. In the United Kingdom the authorities can impose price controls, order the sale of part or all of the business and can render null and void any supplier contracts signed while in breach. Compensation may need to be paid and the cost of any legal activity as a result of the cancelled contracts.

For this reason the EU has published a European Benchmarking Code of Conduct, which largely stems from the work done in the United States, with advice from various bodies connected with benchmarking studies around Europe. In essence the code of conduct above has been expanded and generalised into eight principles:

1. Principle of Preparation.
2. Principle of Contact.
3. Principle of Exchange.
4. Principle of Confidentiality.
5. Principle of Use.
6. Principle of Legality.
7. Principle of Completion.
8. Principle of Understanding and Agreement.

As these guidelines are relatively new, they are unlikely to have been seriously tested in the courts, so there is not, as yet, any legal precedence to go on if you are unsure of whether your data-gathering and process-comparing plan contravenes current competition law. It is always recommended that you seek legal advice if you think a comparison of prices, costings or common suppliers could be misinterpreted by jealous competitors who are not involved in the benchmarking initiative.

multiple benchmarking partners

For the sake of simplicity we have been discussing approaching only one ideal benchmarking partner with whom to compare key processes. In reality you are more likely to be involved with five or six companies, all of whom could mutually benefit from the exercise. It is quite common for organisations to group themselves around a particular functional process and cooperate together to achieve better results. In 1993 Avis, Elida Gibbs, IBM, ICL and Kodak set up a benchmarking group to examine auditing procedures. Although these companies are all global brands, the principle also works for other companies that may not be so well known.

So now that you have understood the etiquette and protocol of what each partner expects, you can legitimately proceed to the stage of making contact.

setting the ground rules and making contact

Now that you have sorted out your list of critical processes and your shortlist of potential benchmarking partners, you may think that the next step is to make some site visits and start comparing performance standards. Wrong.

The next step is the setting of some fairly stringent ground rules, without which you will not get beyond the security gates of your highly desirable benchmarking partner. Setting up that first step in a new relationship, one that could be mutually beneficial for many years to come, needs careful planning.

thinking through your proposition

By this stage you will have arrived at a shortlist of between three and six target companies with whom you are going to compare a specific process or possibly more than one process.

You need to be clear about your choice of partner and what they can provide. Equally you need to be prepared to share your information too. You should bear in mind that however much groundwork has been done, the first site visit may result in aborting the partnership. Things may not be quite as they have been portrayed in the documentation or the trade press.

Assuming you are satisfied that the target partner company has the relevant best-practice process, you should prepare a letter that covers at the very least the following points:

---

1. Brief introduction of your company.
2. Purpose of the approach (to benchmark a critical process).
3. Why you chose the target company.
4. What you can offer in exchange.
5. Parts of the target company you wish to study.
6. The personnel in your team.
7. The length of the site visit(s).

Once this letter is received, it is likely that a series of telephone conversations will take place to clarify the objectives and the best use of the time allotted.

If the target company is aware of the benchmarking concept (almost three-quarters of UK companies claim to benchmark in one form or another), little education will be needed to explain what each partner should expect from the relationship.

If not, some time should be taken, perhaps with a preliminary meeting, to go through the sharing concept, particularly the idea of non-competitive benchmarking. Many worthy partnerships have foundered at this initial stage simply through ignorance.

The final letter, detailing the agenda, people to be visited, background information received, your team and any key issues should be sent in good time so that the target partner can prepare well in advance.

A hastily put together visit, without adequate preparation, will be frustrating for both sides.

Following the principles of Total Quality Management (TQM) it is also a good idea to document all contact, both before and after the site visit, in the event that new management joining midway through the programme can see what has been traded. If the partnership process itself has been documented, you are more likely to get continuing cooperation from a new management team. If it is undocumented and informal, it may be the first activity to be challenged by new owners and all your pioneering work will have been wasted.

be prepared

To get the most of out any benchmarking relationship you need to do some thorough groundwork. Although experienced benchmarkers would say that the most crucial piece of information often comes from a chance remark or random observation on site, there is no substitute for being prepared.

For each department or process you intend to visit you should draft up a questionnaire that details exactly what you want to study, including any relevant statistical reports. Prior to the site visit these questions are likely to be quantitative rather than qualitative. You can ask the 'how' questions when you get there. If possible, try the questionnaire out on your own functional department first, to make sure you are using the right terminology and have understood what they actually do. You could legitimately ask for sample copies of internal forms or written procedures to be sent to you before the visit, in case they throw up other questions and queries.

The data you gather as preparation for the visit can then be compared with your desk research to check for misunderstandings or misinterpretations. With all this direct source data now available you will be able to concentrate during the visit on those parts of the process that are still mysterious and, hopefully, useful to know more about.

site visit day

The big day (or series of days) has arrived. Both partners need to make the most of the opportunity and a general spirit of mutual cooperation will have been developed. But now is the time to stand firm on the overriding objective: to study *how* rather than what or how many. Benchmarking is all about learning how others do similar things better, so you will need to devise beforehand a way to record the answers to lots of how and why questions.

Types of question
How do you achieve this?
Why do/don't you do that?
What is the purpose of this?
Have you always done it that way?
What advantage is there doing it this way?
Do other companies in your field do it like that?
What do your people think about doing it this way?
Is the process documented anywhere?
If it is, does this actually happen in practice?
Which element of the process is key?

Some benchmarkers, with permission, take video cameras and audio recorders so that both the words used and the physical processes undertaken can be thoroughly studied after the visit. Quite often, subtle differences in terms of employee attitude and motivation can be detected in the recording, which perhaps were not immediately apparent during the novelty of the site visit.

It is quite acceptable to ask for quantitative data to support a performance claim, if this data has not already been supplied prior to the visit. But be wary of collecting data for its own sake. Using up valuable database capacity with irrelevant information simply devalues the whole exercise, however impressive the file may look.

exchange protocol

Once again, I am grateful to The Benchmarking Centre for a clear and concise statement of what should or should not be divulged during the data collection stage. The following Benchmarking Exchange Protocol is eminently sensible and will ensure neither party feels disadvantaged when revealing potentially sensitive information.

benchmarking exchange protocol

As the benchmarking process proceeds to the exchange of information, benchmarkers are expected to:

✔ Know and abide by the Benchmarking Code of Conduct.

✔ Have basic knowledge of benchmarking and follow a benchmarking process.

✔ Have determined what to benchmark, identified key performance variables, recognised superior performing companies, and completed a rigorous self-assessment.

✔ Have developed a questionnaire and interview guide, and will share these in advance if requested.

✔ Have the authority to share information.

✔ Work through a specified host and mutually agree on scheduling and meeting arrangements.

✔ Follow these guidelines in face-to-face site visits:

▧ Provide meeting agenda in advance.

▧ Be professional, honest, courteous and prompt.

▧ Introduce all attendees and explain why they are present.

▧ Adhere to the agenda. Maintain focus on benchmarking issues.

■ Use language that is universal, not one's own jargon.
■ Do not share proprietary information without prior approval, from the proper authority, of both parties.
■ Share information about your process, if asked, and consider sharing study results.
■ Offer to set up a reciprocal visit.
■ Conclude meetings and visits on schedule.

one caveat

One of the dynamic characteristics of the benchmarking technique is that instinct and gut feeling should not be ignored. However well prepared you are and however much work you have undertaken in preparation, the initial site visit may lead to aborting the partnership. There could be many reasons, with no blame attached to either side:

1. Clash of cultures (general business approach).
2. Inadequate or unreliable performance data.
3. Management professionalism.
4. 'Feelgood' factor in the relationship.
5. Inappropriate expectations of mutual benefit.

Although such perceptions can be overcome, it is likely that as the exchange of information progresses one or more of these issues will create a stumbling block against genuine cooperation.

It would be better to call a halt early on, than stagger on, only to find 12 months later that neither party has any enthusiasm for the initiative. However, such occurrences are rare if the process of drawing up the shortlist and developing the site visit agenda are followed.

the first report

So, assuming all has gone well, you need to draw up your first report. An initial overview should be conducted in open forum immediately after the visit, so that impressions as well as facts can be established.

A brainstorming type of approach may be a beneficial way to get everything aired and recorded. It is likely that some quantitative information may follow on after some time, to complete the picture of process versus performance.

Drawing up a formal report to include both qualitative and quantitative findings will produce a definitive statement of 'how' and 'why', which was the purpose of the visit. The process maps are particularly important at this stage, as they will be the first elements of comparison and will highlight clearly the big difference between how you do it and how they do it.

In the real world, you may well then compare the process of Company A for a particular task with the process of Company B for the same task, and so on. In this way you can build up a comparative picture of the method that produces the most efficient result.

So, the entire process described above could be done within several other non-competitor companies, provided you are satisfied that the incremental returns are worth the resource expended.

You may also find yourself involved in a similar project for each process being investigated with the attendant workload. You need to ensure that you have enough time to follow through and respond to possible counter-requests from your various benchmarking partners.

your team

Although you may be the champion of benchmarking within your organisation, you are likely to benefit from combining several skill-sets to achieve the best result. You will need to consider what sort of expertise you will be using after the site visit to make sense of what you have seen.

The typical experience you need will be a combination of the following stereotypes:

1. Overall planner, project manager.
2. Statistics, data, process expert.
3. Sympathetic listener.
4. Secretary, recorder.

sorting through the data

There will be a lot of detail to sort through once the first visit is over. It is a good idea to know where it is to be filed, so that it does not gather dust in a corner of the office once you get back. Put the quantitative items together, put the quality comments together, classify any flowcharts or process descriptions in the same place and record any 'surprises' you came across as worthy of further investigation. Questionnaire results gathered pre-inspection and during the inspection should be logged together if they pertain to the same process. It is quite possible that one of your partners has provided you with a lead to find out more about a particular issue that you had not previously investigated. Keep a note of these informal exchanges, as their significance may only become clear at a later date when the data has been thoroughly analysed.

what next?

Creativity and some sharp analysis of data comes next. Now that you have mapped your own key processes and studied successful processes from elsewhere you need to satisfy yourself that the new way of doing things is appropriate for adaptation within your company.

You will also need to unearth the fundamental reasons why your benchmarking partner achieves more efficient results than your company when carrying out a similar process. In other words, you need to find the gap.

finding the performance gap

In broad terms, the eventual aim of all benchmarking techniques is to establish a performance gap. With your competitors, historical information is likely to be numerical (market share, product sales, growth curve, distribution). However, although such 'gap' information is nice to know, it gets you no further in your quest to find *how* they did it to help you do better in the future.

As pointed out in Chapter 1, by the time you get financial information, by definition, it is already out of date. What you really need to know is the efficiency of your systems compared with the efficiency of other systems to do a similar job. If you could compare these systems and their relative results, you would have gained an invaluable insight into improving your company's performance.

Armed with process information from your benchmark partners you can now analyse that performance gap. Finding that 'how' gap is known as process-to-process analysis.

process-to-process analysis

Bob Camp has identified 28 separate tools to help the bench-marking company analyse and compare processes. Not all of them apply to every type of process. But in some cases employing a different but complementary tool can throw light on processes that were previously incomparable.

Use what you think is appropriate to explain the gap in the most straightforward way. Virtuosity in statistical presentation is of no real benefit if your audience does not understand what the diagram is highlighting. Simplicity is the key, if bench-marking is to become an ongoing discipline within your company.

Here are some examples:

Technique		Type of process ratio
Comb chart	→	Customer expectation/actual performance
Histogram	→	Costs of distribution
Matrix	→	Several processes across several companies
Flowchart	→	Customer service sequence
Ishikawa	→	Distribution system dynamics
Spider chart	→	Multiple processes comparison
Scatter diagram	→	Relationship between two variables
Z chart	→	Expenses/revenue ratios
Tree diagram	→	Isolate basic process steps

By experimenting with many different types of performance analysis, you will arrive at a few key methods which, for your company, will create meaningful comparisons on a long-term basis.

Initially there will be 'hard' measures of overall efficiency, culled from desk research and then later verified by site visits.

In time, as an examination of the comparable processes develops, there will be 'soft' measures. There is always a temptation to give less credence to soft measures (perception of service, corporate image, can-do-employee attitude, staff morale), but all soft measures can be indexed to provide hard data.

Provided you are sure that the initial soft measure has been produced with an objective and consistent methodology, comparisons over time can be even more meaningful than financial data as a measure of positive change, especially as we are tracking behavioural improvements. Attitude surveys are a good example of this and many companies rely heavily on quarterly 'morale checks' to time the introduction of sensitive issues.

measuring service: an example

A good example is service provided over the telephone. How good a telephone operator is, at first glance may be a matter of opinion and what day of the week you ring on. But there are many measurable elements of the process you could compare, especially if the operator is both query handler and teleseller.

---

telephone operator measures

Receiving
Length of query-handling call
Number of resolved problems
Reception availability
Quality of advice
Additional services offered
Administration/data reporting
General telephone manner

Outgoing
Number of calls
Sales conversions
Average length of call
Call distribution (by sector)
Follow-up frequency
Referrals
General telephone manner

It could be argued that some of these measures depend on other factors beyond the control of the operator. However, a weighted average of performance across all factors will give a clear and consistent index of how good each operator is, if measurements are taken regularly using the same data-collection methods. Similarly, 'high morale' among employees could be measured by a combination of factors such as attitude surveys, retention, absenteeism, training competence and supervisor appraisals, among many others.

The important discipline is to measure the same things otherwise comparisons over time will become meaningless.

process comparisons in graphic form

Often, the only way to compare a process, quite apart from the performance figure, is to present it in graphic format. Typically, a best, or shall we say better practice, process will have less external influences and will highlight interferences that can be removed (see Figure 8.1).

By removing the elements on the right of the main process (it can be done because your benchmarking partner does it that way), you have identified what you need to do to create a process similar to the best in the market.

tracking the gap

Once you have identified the difference you then need to change your process and measure the difference in performance. In an ideal world the benchmarking partners would stay at the same level of excellence and you would strive to change your processes to narrow the gap (see Figure 8.2).

However, nothing remains the same. The very fact that your partner is a benchmarker means that they will be improving all the time, so the reality of the comparative benchmark situation actually looks like this (see Figure 8.3).

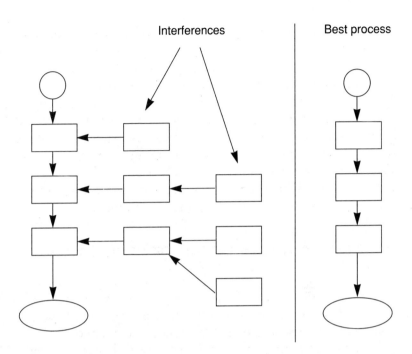

Figure 8.1 *Process-to-process comparison*

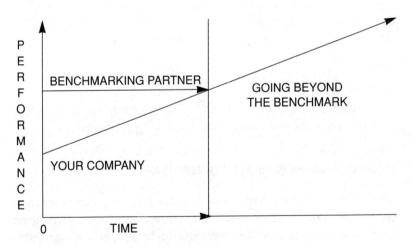

Figure 8.2 *Narrowing the gap*

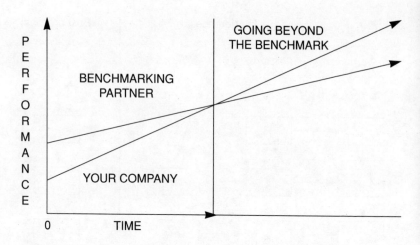

Figure 8.3 *Aim ambitiously – becoming Best In Class*

You need to aim to narrow the gap and assume the benchmarking partner will also be improving, as you improve.

This only goes to show that the essence of benchmarking is continuous improvement. If you surpass the performance of your partner, you would then benchmark against BIC. If you beat the BIC, then you will become the BIC for everyone else to compete against, which is even more of a spur to keep on improving.

As a first-time benchmarker, the key issue to bear in mind is that you will need to set your rate of improvement at an ambitious level, just to keep up with your ever-improving partner. Such is the challenge of true benchmarking partnerships.

performance gap example

One of the satisfying aspects of benchmarking is how practical the results can be. In the example below (Table 8.1), it is clear that your company is the worst of all the benchmarking partners in administrative errors.

Table 8.1   *Error rate per hundred sales transactions*

Company	Percentage	Rank order
A	5.4	Third
B	4.2	First (best)
C	4.8	Second
You	8.4	Fourth (worst)

This presentation of the data not only confirms that you have the worst record in sales administration, it also hints quite strongly that there is a lot to do to improve, as the Best In Class is twice as efficient as your company for this particular process.

what improved processes to adopt first

The net result of all this analysis will be a number of performance standards to aim for and a number of new, improved ways to carry out existing processes. Although in your mind the instant adoption of your discoveries is the obvious route to take, others in the organisation will need time to absorb what you have found and think through the implications of implementation.

It, as if often the case, unnecessary elements of a process can be eliminated, there will be personnel or supplier personnel issues to confront. In addition, changing the way you do things could have a positive or negative influence on costs. Cash flow and capital expenditure budgets may need to be consulted.

A matrix analysis, where processes on the vertical column are compared across your various benchmarking partners on the horizontal column, is usually the best way for non-specialists to spot which processes are the best performing.

Deciding which one would be best for your company is not easy. Would the improvement be short term or long term? Would the improvement be marginal or step change? Would the improvement be easy to implement? Would the improved process look out of place compared with the way the rest of your company does business? After all, there are many ingenious mousetraps, but none so efficient as the wood and wire version.

If you can come to some conclusion, and having examined all of these issues decided which ones to progress, you need to test them with both your internal customer (your departmental sponsor) and, if relevant, your external supplier.

In the final analysis your personnel need to be convinced that your way is a better way. If they cannot be convinced, your new method risks being stillborn. Cooperation is the key. Once this cross-checking has been done, you may come across creative adaptations that to date you had not considered.

When it all comes together and everyone agrees that the new process is the right approach, you have achieved your first major goal: adoption of a new process. The hard part is implementing that new process.

implementing process changes

Implementing change in any organisation is never easy, even if all parties concerned are convinced of the need to change. Benchmarking presents its own unique problems. Personnel will be asked not only to change how they do things but also the way they measure success. Discussions about 'the good old days' may have to be endured during the transition phase for the sake of the future. The inertia factor will be strong, so the management of the implementation of benchmark-driven initiatives will need to be equally robust.

Before you learn the panacea for successful implementation, it is worth considering the likely threats to achievement for first-time benchmarkers.

threats to new process implementation

- Lack of senior-level commitment.
- Lack of resources (cash and manpower).

> ■ No clear results.
> ■ Not enough data.
> ■ Benchmarking team lack of direction.
> ■ Lack of understanding from other personnel.
> ■ Benchmark partner too similar.
> ■ No resultant action taken.
> ■ Benchmarking too many processes.

Each of these threats can be countered with a specific plan. All of them can be covered by adopting a rigorous approach in four areas:

1. Strategic agreement.
2. Team selection and training.
3. Planning.
4. Communication of results.

strategic agreement

Although pressing for a strategic agreement at board level on benchmarking may seem to be overplaying your hand, unless you get high-level agreement you may find yourself continually going cap in hand to budget committees to fund the changes you want to implement.

Equally, other people within the organisation need to see benchmarking as the cornerstone of future profitable growth, not simply a data-collection service. The strategic statement should clearly define that it is the company's aim to seek out best practice and implement similar practices as well as maintaining a monitoring role for the performance of key processes, as indicators of general progress.

Attached to the strategic statement could be a number of clearly defined goals in specific areas, covering the four types of benchmarking (internal, competitive, functional, generic). Action in these areas should be costed into overall budgets and then matched to real results. In benchmarking terms this means a definition of what performance gaps will be analysed, your estimation of how long it will take to close those gaps and how you intend to do it.

The strategic statement leads quickly into a series of tactical activities to support the main statement, but before devising such a plan you should consider who is going to do the work.

team selection and training

With a brand-new company or a company with a relatively small human resources function, you may have the luxury of starting from scratch and building your ideal team. However, the idea of benchmarking usually comes more often in mature organisations looking to create a strategic advantage in a crowded market. In most cases therefore the core of your team may well be sitting around you at this very moment. But if you have a choice, the ideal team should be as follows:

1. Champion team-leader, thoroughly knowledgeable about benchmarking, who can address audiences big and small on its practical implementation as well as its strategic role. Some companies use external consultants in the first instance to spread the knowledge within the organisation, but you should always be considering who will take over the 'internal champion' role, when the consultant has gone.
2. An analyst who can record work processes accurately, keep database information in an orderly fashion and progress-chase various aspects of all your benchmarking initiatives. This team member ought to be fairly dispassionate so that unfettered enthusiasm does not lead the team and the company into implementing unworkable process changes.

Beyond these two essential benchmark team members, you will involve other members on an association basis, as each project develops. if you are studying a specific process, the internal line manager of the current process will undoubtedly need to be privy to the plan, especially the implementation of any gradual or step process changes. In addition you may find a professional benchmarking consultant useful in the early days to help you avoid mistakes and to retain your focus in the crucial early stages.

As with all recruitment issues, training is the key to enhancing the selection choice of specific colleagues. You will need to consider three broad types:

1. Team member(s).
2. Senior managers.
3. Specific functional managers.

team member training

To kick-start the benchmarking programme and get your team up to the mark, external courses provide an efficient way to learn what the words mean and gather some useful technical skills.

There are a number of organisations in the UK that offer a range of highly practical courses, including workshop kits for in-company training, which you can take at your own pace. Many of these courses are modular, designed to be delivered on site in less than 20 hours, and cover such basic skills as analysing processes, collecting data and presenting data, supported by a participants' guide and an instructor's guide.

There is a range of other skill-enhancement mechanisms, from one-day public seminars to video modules, books, case study articles and CD-ROMs.

senior managers

It will be appropriate in the early stages to sell-in the general concept of benchmarking to the senior management group so that when it comes to asking for additional resource, the business case has already been made.

Take care not to spoil the message with too much detail. They should know enough to support departmental initiatives and understand the broad data collection and analytical presentation techniques. Case histories that illustrate specific performance gains are always more compelling than even the most highly crafted philosophical plea. What works and is seen to work gets noticed and subsequently used.

functional managers

Because functional managers will be your first sponsors in any process changes that you make, you need to consider carefully their input and attitude towards benchmarking. Their focus will be on the outcome or result of changing their process rather than the techniques you used to arrive at the answer. Ensure they fully buy into the concept of improvement and the implications of the process change in working practices and manpower needs. Lip service is no good to you when and if you get to implementation stage.

planning

There are a host of books written specifically about task and organisational planning, which it would be foolish to summarise here. Benchmarking does not stand or fall on its logical, analytical approach to real or perceived inefficiencies.

Planning a benchmarking initiative needs to be consistent with normal strategic planning. You should start with a strategic statement or vision of what you expect benchmarking to deliver. You need to attach medium-term goals to that vision, both in activity and result. You should integrate the benchmarking plan into the overall business plan of the organisation. You should isolate a few key initiatives to begin with so that the discipline can earn its spurs and be taken seriously. You can then draw up an operational plan and set short-term achievement goals.

Most benchmarking initiatives take between three and six months to get off the ground, so ensure you do not set your payback dates too early.

A year is a good operational window to start seeing some initial results. Any longer and the sceptic may wonder what all the fuss is about and move to commandeer the budgets for more pressing, short-term problems.

If you have an enlightened senior management team who are immediately convinced that benchmarking is the way forward, you may be able to establish a 'Competency Centre', to deal with all elements of quality. Within this Competency Centre would reside the technical skills and the resource to deliver, internally or externally, a fully functioning quality system. The resource would maintain outside contracts for specific skills/tools or case histories, provide benchmarking training, act as a clearing house to prioritise benchmarking tasks and report on progress to interested parties.

A key element is a benchmarking guide for non-specialists so that line managers and functional managers can apply the techniques in your absence. You may decide that the only way to keep in regular contact with your potential internal sponsors is to set up a network of benchmarking representatives in each business unit who can implement an agreed policy and report back quickly if problems are encountered.

Whatever system of control you implement, someone has to document the work so that changes can be logged in an orderly manner and the resultant efficiencies recorded.

communication

New initiatives will always fight for share of mind in any organisation. However radical the philosophy or concept, once the main idea has been absorbed, it can suffer from fatigue at an early stage, particularly if people perceive it is something human resources are doing in isolation. In other words, there is no real group ownership.

At the heart of a good benchmarking plan is a communication plan, both to reassure the unsure and to underscore any real progress that is taking place.

You need a mechanism to launch the initiative to line managers and the company in general. Depending on your company's size, this may be through team briefings, a corporate video, posters, or a series of internal seminars.

Once the first few projects are up and running you need to drip feed on a systematic basis any efficiency gains made, and encourage those involved in implementing the new process to champion the new way of doing things to other potential internal sponsors.

Regular noticeboard features or articles in the company magazine can help to keep the issue in the forefront of people's minds. Such activity is often planned with the external consultant at the initial stage and launched with a flurry, but then fizzles out as the operational team becomes involved in implementation and the consultant ends his contract.

As the champion of benchmarking, you should examine on a regular basis your communication plan and test from time to time general levels of awareness and understanding through morale checks and employee attitude surveys. Sometimes simply being visible is as important as actually doing the job, particularly if the results will not be known for many months.

Recognition and modest reward are often a good means to getting noticed in a large organisation. Recognition that a process has improved, with subsequent incentive rewards for

those responsible, are effective techniques to keep benchmarking at the top end of the agenda. So take every opportunity you can to promote good benchmarking practice through
formal and informal recognition and reward techniques.
Reinforcing benchmarking behaviour is crucial if the initiative
is going to blossom in Year 2.

top level endorsement

Direct mail specialists will tell you that nothing attracts as
much attention as a good testimonial. Benchmarking is no
exception. Provided you have already obtained top-level
approval, preferably from the CEO, use it unashamedly.

To those familiar with the literature and public relations
aspects of benchmarking, David Kearns, former CEO of Xerox
Corporation, is a recurring source of supportive comment on
the way Xerox has embraced Total Quality Management and
benchmarking in particular. Case history material is full of
quotations from the top person in the company supporting and
endorsing any performance improvement success. It is your
biggest communication asset to gain credibility and ongoing
resources support for what you are trying to achieve.

who should benchmark?

Throughout this brief guide to benchmarking, I have mentioned the value of studying case histories, particularly as benchmarking is such a relatively new performance improvement technique. Seeing how other companies, profit making or non-profit making, approach the spirit of benchmarking can be more illuminating than reading the theory. With this thought in mind and with half an eye, perhaps, to convincing sceptical colleagues that benchmarking is the right way to progress, here are just a few examples of Best In Class companies, taken from a number of sources, who are acknowledged in the *Further Reading* section at the back of this book.

All are well known and there are many detailed examples of their benchmarking successes available in book and magazine formats.

Not all examples need to be so far-reaching in terms of scope and application. A good example is Hawker Fusegear, which is quoted in the *Best Practice Benchmarking Brochure* issued a few years ago by the Department of Trade and Industry. The search for best practice took Tony Tarram, Quality Manager, to a local brickyard where sign-off procedures for new orders

Market sector	BIC company	Process
Financial Services	American Express	Customer service
	Citibank	Technology management
	Sun Life	Empowerment
Automotive	Mercedes Benz	Many aspects
	Lucas Industries	Many aspects
	Nissan	Supplier product development
	Toyota	Many aspects
	Volkswagen	Set-up times
	Honda	Purchasing, empowerment
	Ford	Training
	Harley Davidson	Fleet management
Computing/ Information Technology	IBM	Sales management, among others
	Apple	Inventory control
	Microsoft	Marketing software
	Hewlett Packard	Manufacturing
	Motorola	Quality, product development
	ICL	Product technology
	NEC	Quality systems
	Xerox Corporation	All areas and processes
	AT&T	All areas and processes
	Digital Equipment Corporation	Benchmarking in general
	Canon	Product development
Manufacturing	Hershey Foods	Warehousing, distribution
	NCR	Purchasing
	Philip Morris	Manufacturing
	Westinghouse	Stock control
	Siemens Plessey	Benchmarking in general
	Elida Fabergé	Innovation
	Milliken	All aspects

that were easy to audit were introduced in a modified format to Hawker Fusegear, with 'a massive reduction in errors'.

Further examples of benchmarking success (and who was responsible for them) can come from subscription-based benchmarking club magazines, which include such topics as improving core competencies, benchmarking dos and don'ts, supply-chain benchmarking, managing the internal transfer of best practice and international trends. Case history material from AT&T, Baxter Healthcare, BP Oil, Cable & Wireless, Deutsche Aerospace, Du Pont, Rover, HMSO, Bristol-Myers, Thorn Lighting and Philips has appeared in club magazines.

Another source of case histories comes from industry associations who are paid by member companies to gather information on their behalf so that they can improve similar process performance. The Printed Circuit Interconnection Federation (PCIF) represents the interests of the electronics interconnection and packaging companies. They benchmark competing companies across several manufacturing processes so that members can measure their own performance. The Society of British Aerospace Companies (SBAC) benchmarks best practice in processes to do with cycling time reduction and Just in Time (JIT) manufacturing, among many others.

There are several sources of financial benchmarking information typified by Companies House or credit-rating organisations like Dun & Bradstreet in the UK where you can measure your financial performance against your direct competitors in minute detail.

An innovative service to its industry by a trade magazine, rather than an association, comes from *Meetings and Incentive Travel* (Conference and Incentive Travel Publications), which publishes each year, at no cost to the trade readership, a financial benchmarks survey of around 40 companies who compete in the corporate conferences and meetings industry. Clearly such information does not explain how each company achieved the financial ratios highlighted, but competitive, financial benchmarking is better than no benchmarking at all.

anyone can benchmark

Although it is always uplifting to read case histories of how major, well-known companies undertook a particular benchmarking initiative and improved their efficiency, small companies can do it too. If your task is to get the technique accepted as part of the annual business plan, examples from large organisations can help you gain credibility for the usage of the technique. But benchmarking can work equally well on a smaller scale. Simply by taking more notice of your critical processes, it is possible to create benchmarking partnerships without the formality of a club or benchmarking clearing house, and you do not have to be a corporate executive.

A local newsagent worried about customer service could contact his local branch of Marks & Spencer and ask to observe best-practice customer care. Local discretion may allow the newsagent sight of the Marks & Spencer Customer Service training manual, which could provide guidelines. Very little process analysis or documentation would be produced but the spirit of learning from others who are demonstrably better is evident.

The technique may need to become more formalised in the case of, say, a small group of independent, regional car dealers who may wish to measure their overall financial ratios and service retention against other similar dealers. The personnel manager may be the designated benchmarking team leader who can draw on many of his supporting motor manufacturers for help and guidance through the manufacturer's zone representative. Beyond this level, it would then be appropriate to adopt a more formal approach, along the lines described in this brief overview of benchmarking.

universal application

Unlike many business improvement techniques requiring a

critical mass to be effective, benchmarking can be applied across a wide range of companies, big or small, at minimal cost. From the corner shop to the multinational, anyone can benchmark, with a little ingenuity and creativity.

The essence of the technique is examining how you carry out your most important processes and finding out if they can be done better in the future. So in answer to the question, 'Who should benchmark?', the answer is, everyone can.

11

Kaizen: the continuous improvement philosophy

> 'Kaizen means ongoing improvement involving everyone – top management, managers and workers.' Masaaki Imai, populariser of Kaizen in the West.

Whenever two or three practitioners of benchmarking are gathered together, as the saying goes, the conversation turns inevitably to Kaizen (pronounced 'ky-zen'). If you are serious about becoming the champion for benchmarking in your organisation, you need to know a little about this Japanese business concept. This chapter deals with what Kaizen is and how it is applied.

so what is Kaizen?

If benchmarking is the technique for measuring improvement and identifying performance gaps, Kaizen is the overall philosophy of gradual and systematic improvement. In Japan, the word Kaizen is all-pervasive and means 'good-change' or improvement.

Many spheres of Japanese life have a Kaizen element: education, economics, agriculture, even sport. Television newscasters talk about the Kaizen of international diplomacy, political development and industrial relations. It is often said that Kaizen is what distinguishes the performance of Western businesses from Japanese businesses.

Whereas most successful companies in the West are driven by a relatively short-term profit motive from a step change, Japanese companies take the gradual improvement view when deciding how much to invest. If a new idea or a different process cannot deliver instant incremental margins, a Western business tends not to invest, in favour of step changes that will deliver quicker bottom-line returns.

In Japan, the Kaizen philosophy means the emphasis is always on process improvement on a gradual basis because improved processes will produce better profitability in the medium and long term. It is the difference between process-oriented management and results-oriented management.

what does Kaizen look like?

In its most simple form, it could be a suggestion scheme, but not the stale, tired programmes dying of neglect you often find languishing in Western businesses.

Kaizen-inspired suggestion schemes form an integral part of most successful Japanese businesses. Supervisors are measured on their ability to produce large numbers of process-improvement suggestions from their directly reporting employees. The

UK Association of Suggestion Schemes keeps records of the average number of suggestions put forward by UK-registered scheme employees. W H Smith, in one year, produced 2551 ideas from 34,052 employees. Abbey National produced 1537 ideas from 17,000 employees during the same period.

Toyota, in Japan, produces 1.5 million suggestions a year, of which 95 cent are applied in some form. The difference is accounted for by the fact that everyone's job has a Kaizen element, from board director to lowliest employee. At least 50 per cent of a Japanese manager's time is spent on 'improvement'.

Such a disparity in achievement cannot be explained away by the lack of a benchmarking programme. The figures highlight the different approaches to the delivery of quality between most Eastern and Western firms. In the West ideas for improvement are usually submitted on an individual basis up the management line, with rewards being given to the individual author. In the East improvement ideas are normally discussed within the work group and modified until the group is happy with the results. Ideas are then costed by the group, using outside specialists if necessary for assessing how they will ultimately benefit the customer. The team conducts a pilot test over a meaningful period with the agreement of the line manager. If and only if an idea delivers an improvement in the process will it be adopted. At that stage the whole team is recognised for its work and the originator is afforded special recognition.

Programmes are in place to practise Kaizen in small groups through quality circles, think-sessions and group incentive schemes as well as individual systems to help improve self-development and promote a more fulfilled working day.

One of the key focus areas for Kaizen is waste in all its forms. Just In Time (JIT) delivery of components for a manufacturing process comes directly from the drive to eliminate waste. What waste, you may ask?

1. Overproduction
2. Time at the machine
3. Transporting units
4. Process time
5. Stock checking
6. Physical movement of stock
7. Defective stock replacement

A similar approach can be made to virtually all manager–employee relations. Time-consuming personal reviews, responsibility sign-off, interviews, and regular formal supervising are all manifestations of management time-wasting that could be eliminated through changing the management process.

One of the most distinctive differences between West and East in business is management style. Whereas most Japanese supervisors encourage an open door, walkabout policy, with direct contact between the management cadre and the shop floor, in the West such practices are rarely widespread (although we are learning fast). We prefer the employee to come to the office at a specific time (regardless of his or her schedule) to be given instructions or advised on policy.

Managers in Japan are measured on their capacity to *improve* the work processes for which they are responsible. Workers are measured by their ability to *maintain* those processes and keep them in good running order. Both have a duty to search for better, more efficient ways to do the overall corporate task.

Warusa Kagen

This obsession with improvement leads to another collaborative concept that is universally evident in Japan – Warusa Kagen. Employees are taught to anticipate defective processes, long before they happen, so that small problems do not become big problems later on. Workers are encouraged to report to their supervisors if things are 'not quite right'! Far from being criticised for complaining, such an attitude is welcomed, provided it can be quantified.

There are many problem processes that go unaltered for years in many businesses in the West because they are felt to be trivial or nit-picking. Over the years such inefficiency can build up into a major problem that could have been avoided by more open reporting concepts.

The most useful application of Warusa Kagen is between departments or functions where most process difficulties in organisations are noticed (marketing versus sales, research versus marketing, distribution versus finance) but because of departmental pride and protectionism tend to remain unanalysed.

introducing Kaizen into Western organisations

This is a tall order. Kaizen is part of Japanese culture, not Western work culture. However, there are some useful technical disciplines that can encourage the Kaizen attitude to be nurtured and grow. These techniques are: the five whys, the five Ms, the five Ss and the three Mus.

the five whys

If part of a process is defective or perceived to be so, you need to ask why five times, taking the investigation one step further with each question. For example:

This machine coffee is cold.
Why?
Because the heating element burns out after 50,000 cups.
Why?
Because better elements are too expensive.
Why?

Because they all have to be imported.
Why?
Because we do not have the cost-effective technology here.
Why?
Because labour is too expensive.

After just five whys, you can see that the debate about the many processes in this apparently simple task could range from distribution and technology of heating elements to a new marketing and manufacturing opportunity (making better heating elements in the UK).

the five Ms

The five Ms stand for man, machine, material, method and measurement. Each heading provides the opportunity to ask 10 questions about each 'M' of the process to see if improvements could be made. For example:

method (of operation)

1. Is it safe?
2. Is it efficient?
3. Is the standard adequate?
4. Is the environment a factor?
5. Is the set-up adequate?
6. How does this process fit into place with other processes?
7. Does it produce consistent quality?
8. Is there adequate lighting and ventilation?
9. Can the method be easily taught to others?
10. Can the work standard be improved?

the five Ss

The five Ss are taken from the initial letters of five Japanese words:

Seiri: to straighten up
Prepare the machine/process and discard unnecessary tools.

Seiton: to put things in order
All tools should be put in the right order in the sequence of the process so that no time is wasted looking for the correct equipment during the operation.

Seiso: to clean up
Clean up the working area before the task and as you go along.

Seiketsu: to keep oneself clean
Keeping yourself clean and tidy helps to foster a clean and tidy attitude to the work process.

Shitsuke: to maintain discipline
All procedures should be followed, as they will be the best current practice (unless our Kaizen instinct can suggest a few improvements).

Clearly some of these ideas may be common practice in industrial manufacturing, but try applying the five Ss to an administrative job and the implications may be enlightening. (How many of us start to make a telephone call without preparing ourselves adequately with the correct data, or anticipate the likely response?)

the three Mus

The three Mus stand for Muda (waste), Muri (strain) and Mura (discrepancy). For many manufacturing businesses the

three Mus checklist can be a useful aide-memoire in promoting
Warusa Kagen – to use the jargon.

Resource	Muda	Muri	Mura
Manpower	✔	✗	✔
Technique	✔	✔	✔
Method	✗	✔	✗
Time	✗	✔	✗
Facility	✗	✗	✔
Jigs/Tools	✔	✔	✗
Materials	✔	✔	✔
Production volume	✗	✔	✗
Inventory	✗	✗	✔
Place	✔	✗	✗
Way of thinking	✔	✔	✗

Using this checklist, processes can be given a swift health check
and point the way to corrective action by specialists or the
team itself.

the benefits of Kaizen

It goes without saying that improvement makes sense. The
problem is that it often goes unimplemented in many organisations in the West, which leads to no improvement at all.
Workers are not encouraged to report defects or suggest a
change to current practice. Managers tend to copy their prede-
cessors in terms of management style, so habits learnt from the
generation of the Industrial Revolution still prevail in many
businesses.

By adopting the philosophy of Kaizen, with very little capital
outlay, many organisations in the West could produce dramatic

increases in productivity. Thirty to fifty per cent increases are not unusual with those who have introduced Kaizen techniques for the first time. Because Kaizen includes workers as well as management, everyone can participate for the greater good. Part of the concept is the rewarding of effort not just results and the training of everyone in the simple questioning techniques (see above) to lay bare every single process in the business on a continual basis.

Japanese Kaizen case histories contain many examples of individual and group recognition and reward programmes to help reinforce Kaizen behaviour.

Real benefits ensure:

1. Everyone grasps the real issues more quickly.
2. More emphasis on planning and prevention develops.
3. Process and quality replace cost and results.
4. Effort is concentrated on what matters.
5. Everyone participates in building the business.

learning more about Kaizen

This chapter has been nothing more than a brief description of the Kaizen concept. To learn more, read *Kaizen – The Key to Japan's Competitive Success* by Masaaki Imai, who has worked both in Japan and the West as a business consultant. It contains many working examples of the Kaizen concept and the effect it has had on numerous successful Japanese businesses.

Since the end of the Second World War, Japan – and the Far East in general – has been able to assimilate the technology and best practices of the West, most notably from the United States, and produce world-beating business performance. Much of this success is the ingrained work ethic of Kaizen – gradual process improvement – exhibited by oriental management as well as their workers.

It has often been said that large Western organisations can only now survive and grow through flexible response systems and a workforce obsessed with quality. Kaizen, and its hand-maiden, benchmarking, could deliver that mission, if only more people were aware of the benefits that such performance improvement techniques can generate.

benchmarking and quality

Benchmarking is a practical discipline but is only a means to an end. By itself, the techniques described will do nothing more than draw a line in the corporate sand to say, 'We are here and our competitors are over there'. The performance standards that regular benchmarking uncovers need to lead to action. It is part of the journey toward higher quality. It is worth considering, therefore, how benchmarking fits in with the concept of quality, if only to see it in perspective. The best practitioner of benchmarking in the world is no better off if no action is taken as a result of what is discovered.

Total Quality Management (TQM)

When the issue of quality first comes up in most organisations, the instant reaction may be to enrol senior people on a TQM course. Total Quality Management has become in recent years the perceived panacea for business stagnation. But what exactly is it?

TQM is the generic term for a collection of techniques that, when applied, lead to a consistent standard of product or service appropriate to the customer. The techniques tend to cover three main areas:

1. Management.
2. Process.
3. Customer interface.

The quality approach to management behaviour may involve such issues as teamwork, equipment, employee involvement, rapid learning, recognition, communication and participation. Within these areas the role of the management team is to emphasise customer needs (internal and external), to create synergy within teams and between departments and to implement measurement systems so that performance and output can be recognised and rewarded.

We have discussed the improvement of quality processes elsewhere in this book. The process element of TQM is crucial if the organisation is to become efficient. TQM areas within process management could include process analysis, metrics, prevention, cost reduction, waste and all the many elements in the added-value chain that makes one organisation better than its rivals.

The third aspect of TQM focuses on the customer. Satisfaction surveys, service ethics, matching needs and continuous review of customer experience (either real or perceived) could all be part of a TQM initiative.

Once you get into the detail of TQM, other terms are used to describe specific approaches, but the overall philosophy of quality and how to achieve it is TQM. There are many approaches to moving a business from the TQM concept to everyday reality. One well-known business concept writer on the topic of quality is Philip Crosby, who defines quality as 'conformance to requirements' and is often quoted with reference to 'zero defects' (ie ultimate quality is a product with no defects).

In a more philosophic vein, the late W E Deming (who first taught Japanese industrialists how to measure output scientifically) concentrated his quality thinking on the role of the employee. His 14 management guidelines for creating quality cover many of the current initiatives and techniques we use today to build up to an integrated quality plan.

Bill Conway, another incisive thinker about quality, emphasises six tools for quality improvement, which tend to rely on data collection and analysis.

Conway's tools for quality improvement

1. Human relation skills.
2. Statistical surveys.
3. Simple statistical presentation.
4. Statistical process control.
5. Engineering.
6. Industrial Engineering.

More recently, the Japanese expert and consultant Shigeo Shingo specialises in systems that deliver 'perfect' products through zero quality control and devices to catch errors upstream in the production process, rather than letting them be inspected out later. He is the developer of 'Poka-Yoke' or foolproofing, which provides a checklist for the operative of every conceivable error that could occur, so as to potentially eliminate human error.

Every expert has a slightly different approach depending on the economic environment and era in which they worked. However, it was inevitable that sooner or later a standard approach would emerge.

European Foundation for Quality Management (EFQM)

The EFQM was founded in 1988 by 14 chief executives of leading European companies to consolidate their various quality approaches and thereby be better armed to defend their corporate position in their increasingly global markets. The organisation now has well over 400 corporate members across Europe.

Their aim is twofold:

1. To support Western European management teams in the development of quality initiatives to achieve global competitive advantage.
2. To enhance the quality culture of Europe as a whole.

One of the main public relations activities of the EFQM is the European Quality Award (EQA). Each year the EFQM recognises outstanding achievement in corporate quality as a model for others to aim towards.

Winners since the award structure was established in 1992 include Rank Xerox, Milliken, and D2D, a distribution subsidiary of ICL.

A similar organisation and award system operates within the UK, known as the British Quality Foundation, which exists to promote the adoption of TQM practices. Rover Group, as it was then known, and TNT jointly received the first Quality Award in 1994.

Both organisations publish a model for initiating and implementing quality throughout an organisation with points being awarded for performance in each section. Figure 12.1 is an illustration of the EFQM model, in outline.

It is clear from the headings in Figure 12.1 that TQM is meant to be an all-embracing concept where no element of an organisation is left untouched in the search for better quality.

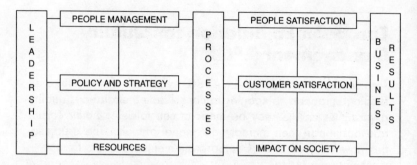

Figure 12.1 *EFQM model*

ISO 9000 and its derivatives

An important catalyst in moving an organisation towards quality processes is the establishment of efficient systems that you can then begin to benchmark. The International Standards Organisation (ISO) introduced a framework for establishing quality standards to which organisations could aspire. Five levels were set up in 1987, which could be followed as a practical guideline to establish quality.

ISO 9000	General guidelines
ISO 9001/2	Establishing Quality Assurance
ISO 9003/4	Total Quality Systems

As a framework the ISO 9000 series is a practical aid to getting started down the road to quality and provides a measurable action plan once the general principle of TQM has been understood and embraced.

In essence ISO 9004 is a never-ending approach to improving quality, with practical self-assessment measures to deliver the Kaizen philosophy of continuous improvement. Benchmarking would be an active element of ISO 9004.

The Malcolm Baldridge National Quality Award

As most benchmarking case histories emanate from the USA, you should be aware of the Malcolm Baldridge National Quality Award. The MBNQA is the American equivalent of the EQA (see above) but has been in existence since 1987. Applications have grown steadily since inception and among performance improvement enthusiasts it is the top award for excellence in quality. There are seven core values that are benchmarked.

MBNQA Core Values	Points
1. Leadership	90
2. Information and analysis	80
3. Strategic quality planning	60
4. Human resources development	150
5. Process quality management	140
6. Quality and operational results	180
7. Customer focus and satisfaction	300
	1000

As benchmarking and its associated quality ethos become more widespread, such public methods of recognition will develop to encourage more companies to aspire to higher standards.

the role of benchmarking

Within all the above systems for delivering and recognising quality, benchmarking plays a key role in *underpinning* performance. Quality can neither be established nor improved without basic benchmarking techniques. Someone, somewhere, has to roll up their shirtsleeves and get down to collecting data and comparing processes.

It is therefore vital to recognise the highly practical nature of benchmarking, when discussing the finer points of Crosby, Deming, TQM and ISO 9000. A thorough knowledge of benchmarking can deliver the vision of performance improvement writers in a logical, simple format.

how benchmarking fits in

In broad terms then, TQM is the overall concept, Kaizen is the drive within TQM for continuous improvement, EFQM provides the framework for a corporate action strategy, ISO 9000 establishes a measurable standard, and benchmarking underpins the entire initiative by collecting and analysing relevant process data to compare with process data from other organisations (see Figure 12.2).

The route to superior quality and market leadership ends with the overriding philosophy of TQM, but the beginning of the journey, setting the standard for improvement, is benchmarking.

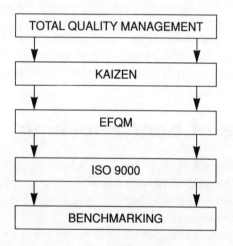

Figure 12.2 *How benchmarking fits in*

the future of benchmarking

If you are just starting down the benchmarking road, you may not be interested at this stage in what lies beyond benchmarking. After all, you have only just learnt the principles of this valuable business improvement technique. You may feel that looking over and beyond the horizon is a little premature.

However, to complete your understanding of the overall concept you should be aware of what mature benchmarking companies are thinking, if only to shave a few more points off that all-important performance gap between them and you in the years to come.

According to a survey of businesses in the UK, best-practice benchmarking was little known as a management technique in 1990. It was a novel and stimulating topic but there was a general lack of awareness surrounding it.

Going back five more years to 1985, in the USA, there was only a handful of companies out of the *Fortune 500* actively applying benchmarking techniques. Today every multinational is either investigating or applying benchmarking skills to retain their competitive edge on a global basis. You are in good company if you are only just investigating what benchmarking can offer.

However, companies that have used benchmarking techniques over the last decade to great effect can suffer from one major disadvantage: institutionalisation. Benchmarking for some companies may have been overplayed, leading to lack of enthusiasm in the face of other business pressures, or undercommunicated because they feel everyone is familiar with the topic.

In an organisation that has been successful all over the world, there may be a tendency to lose the basic humility that goes with recognising that somewhere out there someone is doing things better than you. Within such companies, new blood has to be brought in to take over the pioneering work of the initial instigators of benchmarking. Customer- and supplier-focus groups could provide the new ideas and stimulus to looking at the world through the other end of the telescope: in other words, through the eyes of the consumer.

Communications should be constantly reviewed. Changing the methods and style of communications will create renewed interest in the topic of benchmarking.

Don't forget that new recruits to your organisation will need to be trained in the ways of the benchmarking ethos and the philosophy of Kaizen.

Developments on the Internet, and the increasing usage of extranets and intranets makes the exchange of information much easier and is likely to accelerate the number of benchmarking partnerships that are set up.

The future of benchmarking is elusive. If benchmarking is to be defined as continuous improvement, then benchmarking as a technique will, by definition, go on forever.

There is no doubt that all organisations could be slicker at collecting and exchanging information. Improvements in computer software to help compare processes would be very useful, allowing more time to consider the differences rather than spending that time merely building ever more accurate representations on paper or on screen. To some extent we are all constrained by the amount we are prepared to invest in new technology for information exchange.

Some commentators argue that what hampers the development of benchmarking most is the lack of process classification. In other words, process-to-process analysis would be much easier if all businesses used the same terminology when describing similar or indeed the same processes. Much time at present can be wasted on describing a process in detail only to find it is in fact exactly the same as a competitor process, under a different name.

If the day came when every organisation benchmarked as a matter of course, just as every organisation in modern times draws up a balance sheet or has a remuneration policy, the operators of the benchmarking programmes would be able to compare ever more marginal processes, providing that additional competitive edge, however small. Kaizen would become a working reality.

As organisations develop, and performance today – exemplified by efficient processes – becomes as important a yardstick as performance yesterday – measured by financial ratios – we can imagine a performance director at board level reporting and advising on better processes with as much clout as today's financial director who finds the cash to fund it.

The speed of technological change is such that it will become increasingly more difficult to keep up with process improvements as gathering the data and mapping a process generally happen more slowly in most organisations than implementing new ways of doing things.

The backlog of processes to analyse means there is a real need for a universal database of processes so that benchmarking members can update themselves quickly on new ideas, preferably on screen, on a worldwide basis.

There is no doubt that Total Quality Management (TQM) and Business Process Re-engineering (BPR) will be refined in due course and become ever more specific, which comes with the maturity of a business concept.

At the heart of these performance-improvement philosophies there will always be the need to collect the relevant data, make a comparison and instigate a better way. Benchmarking encompasses that basic discipline. It may happen 10 times faster in the 21st century, but it will still be benchmarking.

Benchmarking excellence in the future will come about through more skilled people who are better trained; networked electronic data that can be easily compared; and more senior managers who recognise that world-class quality can only be delivered through measuring processes rather than bottom line results. Measuring processes means applying benchmarking techniques.

your mission

So now you know all about benchmarking. Or at least you may know just a little more than before you bought this book. Your mission is to become the benchmarking champion for your company, familiarise yourself with the case histories, the hands-on techniques and the process analysis tools.

But when all the studying is over and the information has been collected, and the people have been trained, someone has to make it happen in your organisation. Will it be you?

Good luck and good benchmarking.

further reading

Camp, R C (1989) *Benchmarking: The search for best practices that lead to superior performance*, ASQC Quality Press, Milwaukee.

Camp, R C (1995) *Business Process Benchmarking*, ASQC Quality Press, Milwaukee.

Cook, Sarah (1995) *Practical Benchmarking*, Kogan Page, London.

Imai, Masaaki (1986) *Kaizen – The Key to Japan's Competitive Success*, McGraw–Hill, New York.

Reider, Rob (2000) *Benchmarking Strategies*, John Wiley & Sons, New York.

Zairi, Dr M (1992) *Competitive Benchmarking: An executive guide*, Technical Communications (Publishing) Ltd, reprinted 1994, Stanley Thornes, Cheltenham.

Zairi, Dr M (1996) *Benchmarking for Best Practice*, Reed Educational and Professional Publishing; reprinted 1999 by Butterworth–Heinemann.

Visit Kogan Page on-line

Comprehensive information on
Kogan Page titles

Features include

- complete catalogue listings,
  including book reviews and
  descriptions

- on-line discounts on a variety
  of titles

- special monthly promotions

- information and discounts on
  NEW titles and BESTSELLING titles

- a secure shopping basket facility
  for on-line ordering

- infoZones, with links and
  information on specific areas of
  interest

PLUS everything you need to know
about KOGAN PAGE

http://www.kogan-page.co.uk